1st EDITION

Perspectives on Diseases and Disorders

Chronic Fatigue Syndrome

Sylvia Engdahl
Book Editor

GALE
CENGAGE Learning™

Detroit • New York • San Francisco • New Haven, Conn • Waterville, Maine • London

Elizabeth Des Chenes, *Managing Editor*

© 2012 Greenhaven Press, a part of Gale, Cengage Learning

Gale and Greenhaven Press are registered trademarks used herein under license.

For more information, contact:
Greenhaven Press
27500 Drake Rd.
Farmington Hills, MI 48331-3535
Or you can visit our Internet site at gale.cengage.com

For product information and technology assistance, contact us at

Gale Customer Support, 1-800-877-4253
For permission to use material from this text or product, submit all requests online at
www.cengage.com/permissions

Further permissions questions can be e-mailed to permissionrequest@cengage.com

Articles in Greenhaven Press anthologies are often edited for length to meet page requirements. In addition, original titles of these works are changed to clearly present the main thesis and to explicitly indicate the author's opinion. Every effort is made to ensure that Greenhaven Press accurately reflects the original intent of the authors. Every effort has been made to trace the owners of copyrighted material.

Cover image AMA/Shutterstock.com

LIBRARY OF CONGRESS CATALOGING-IN-PUBLICATION DATA

Chronic fatigue syndrome / Sylvia Engdahl, book editor.
   p. cm. -- (Perspectives on diseases and disorders)
  Includes bibliographical references and index.
  Summary: "Perspectives on Diseases and Disorders: Chronic Fatigue Syndrome: Understanding Chronic Fatigue Syndrome; Controversies Surrounding Chronic Fatigue Syndrome; Personal Narratives"--Provided by publisher.
  ISBN 978-0-7377-5773-6 (hardback)
 1. Chronic fatigue syndrome. I. Engdahl, Sylvia. II. Series: Perspectives on diseases and disorders.
  [DNLM: 1. Fatigue Syndrome, Chronic. WB 146]
  RB150.F37C4734 2011
  616'.0478--dc23

                              2011013457

Printed in the United States of America
1 2 3 4 5 6 7 15 14 13 12 11

CONTENTS

FOREWORD

"Medicine, to produce health, has to examine disease."
—Plutarch

Independent research on a health issue is often the first step to complement discussions with a physician. But locating accurate, well-organized, understandable medical information can be a challenge. A simple Internet search on terms such as "cancer" or "diabetes," for example, returns an intimidating number of results. Sifting through the results can be daunting, particularly when some of the information is inconsistent or even contradictory. The Greenhaven Press series Perspectives on Diseases and Disorders offers a solution to the often overwhelming nature of researching diseases and disorders.

From the clinical to the personal, titles in the Perspectives on Diseases and Disorders series provide students and other researchers with authoritative, accessible information in unique anthologies that include basic information about the disease or disorder, controversial aspects of diagnosis and treatment, and first-person accounts of those impacted by the disease. The result is a well-rounded combination of primary and secondary sources that, together, provide the reader with a better understanding of the disease or disorder.

Each volume in Perspectives on Diseases and Disorders explores a particular disease or disorder in detail. Material for each volume is carefully selected from a wide range of sources, including encyclopedias, journals, newspapers, nonfiction books, speeches, government documents, pamphlets, organization newsletters, and position papers. Articles in the first chapter provide an authoritative, up-to-date overview that covers symptoms, causes and effects, treatments, cures, and medical advances. The second chapter presents a substantial number of opposing viewpoints on controversial treatments and other current debates relating to the volume topic. The third chapter offers a variety of personal perspectives on the disease or disorder. Patients, doctors, caregivers, and loved ones represent just some of the voices found in this narrative chapter.

Each Perspectives on Diseases and Disorders volume also includes:

- An **annotated table of contents** that provides a brief summary of each article in the volume.
- An **introduction** specific to the volume topic.
- Full-color **charts and graphs** to illustrate key points, concepts, and theories.
- Full-color **photos** that show aspects of the disease or disorder and enhance textual material.
- **"Fast Facts"** that highlight pertinent additional statistics and surprising points.
- A **glossary** providing users with definitions of important terms.
- A **chronology** of important dates relating to the disease or disorder.
- An annotated list of **organizations to contact** for students and other readers seeking additional information.
- A **bibliography** of additional books and periodicals for further research.
- A detailed **subject index** that allows readers to quickly find the information they need.

Whether a student researching a disorder, a patient recently diagnosed with a disease, or an individual who simply wants to learn more about a particular disease or disorder, a reader who turns to Perspectives on Diseases and Disorders will find a wealth of information in each volume that offers not only basic information, but also vigorous debate from multiple perspectives.

INTRODUCTION

Chronic fatigue syndrome (CFS) is an illness with a misleading name—a name that most patients dislike and would like to see changed. It gives people the wrong impression about the disorder. While it is true that people with CFS suffer from persistent fatigue that makes normal activity impossible and is not relieved by rest, their condition is not just a matter of feeling tired. There are many other symptoms, such as muscle and joint pain, unrefreshing sleep, and sometimes headaches, sore throat, and swollen lymph glands. In some cases they also have cognitive dysfunction that interferes with concentration and even memory. But because they do not look sick, other people generally do not understand how ill they are.

Some people prefer the name chronic fatigue and immune dysfunction syndrome (CFIDS). In Canada, Britain and Europe, however, myalgic encephalomyelitis (ME) is the name most often used, and because it suggests the seriousness of the illness, patients and their supporters strongly advocate adopting it in the United States. Therefore, the term "ME/CFS" is starting to replace CFS, and in October 2010 the Chronic Fatigue Syndrome Advisory Committee of the US Department of Health and Human Services unanimously endorsed a recommendation to make it official. The Centers for Disease Control and Prevention, which introduced the name "chronic fatigue syndrome" in the first place, has not made this change, but it may do so in the future.

The cause of ME/CFS is not known, and there are as yet no laboratory tests that can detect its presence; it is diagnosed only by ruling out other possible causes of the symptoms. For this reason, some doctors have maintained it is not a real illness, although this view is gradually changing. A fierce controversy exists within the medical profession about whether ME/CFS is a biological disorder or merely a psychological one. Since doctors tend to see things in the light of their own specialties, physicians who are interested in the illness generally look for biochemical explanations, while psychiatrists maintain that it is of psychological origin. Most experts believe that both biological and psychological factors are probably involved.

In considering this controversy, it is important to understand that the term "psychological" has different meanings to different people. Although some doctors have used the term to mean "all in the head," i.e., imaginary; those who are knowledgeable about the subject no longer do so. Few if any medical authorities now think it is an imaginary illness. Some, however, including many psychiatrists, think it is a matter of experiencing real physical symptoms as the result of a psychological disorder, something that can and does happen in individual cases of other illnesses. This is known as *somatization*, and one of the theories about why it occurs is that a person's unconscious mind may affect the body in such a way as to produce physical symptoms in lieu of emotional distress.

Most experts believe that chronic fatigue syndrome is caused by both biological and psychological factors. (© Blickwinkel/Alamy)

The debate about whether CFS is of psychological or biological origin may be merely a reflection of insufficient knowledge about how psychological and physical effects normally interact. For example, scientists have known since the 1980s, when the science of psychoneuroimmunology was founded, that psychological factors can weaken the immune system; this is a *normal* reaction of the body that was discovered through experiments with animals. It is generally thought that the immune system is in some way involved in ME/CFS. Therefore, it could be that the effects of emotional stress on the immune system result in the body's vulnerability to attack by an infection-causing agent, such as a virus.

Viruses have long been suspected of playing a role in ME/CFS, and one after another, specific ones have been ruled out. But in 2009 a new virus, XMRV, was found in the blood of a large percentage of the ME/CFS patients studied, causing great excitement among patients as well as researchers. This was confirmed in 2010, and as this book goes to press, more research is under way to settle the debate about conflicting results from different studies. Although XMRV alone cannot explain ME/CFS—since it has also been found in the blood of people with prostate cancer and that of healthy individuals—it may prove to be a biological marker that would allow at least some forms of the illness to be diagnosed through laboratory testing. And if the virus contributes to any disease, steps can be taken to keep it from spreading. Because of the possibility that it may, the American Red Cross announced in December 2010 that people with ME/CFS will no longer be allowed to donate blood.

Patients hope that XMRV will be shown to cause ME/CFS because that would put an end to the theory that it is the result of a psychological disorder. They point out that other serious diseases, such as multiple sclerosis and even diabetes, were considered psychological in nature before the discovery of their biochemical bases. Whether or not the association between XMRV and ME/CFS turns out to be causal, research into its significance will continue.

CHAPTER 1

Understanding Chronic Fatigue Syndrome

An Overview of Chronic Fatigue Syndrome

Toni Rizzo

Chronic fatigue syndrome (CFS) has had several different names because no one knows what causes it, and various other conditions have similar symptoms. These symptoms last for six months or longer and are far more serious than ordinary fatigue; they leave people unable to work or perform normal daily activities. In the following viewpoint writer Toni Rizzo says that some doctors think CFS is a psychological disorder, although many scientists believe it may be triggered by a virus. Researchers now think that it is not a single illness and that not all cases have the same cause. There is no cure, and many patients never regain their health, but treatments are available to relieve some of the symptoms. Rizzo specializes in science and medical writing.

Photo on previous page. A young woman with myalgic encephalomyelitis is pictured here. This disorder—as well as other conditions—often occurs in individuals having CFS. (© Tim Caddick/Alamy)

Chronic fatigue syndrome (CFS) is a condition that causes extreme tiredness. People with CFS have debilitating fatigue that lasts for six months or longer. They also have many other symptoms. Some of these are pain in the joints and muscles, headache, and

SOURCE: Toni Rizzo, "Chronic Fatigue Syndrome," *Gale Encyclopedia of Medicine.* Gale, 2006. Copyright © 2006 by Gale. Reproduced by permission of Gale, a part of Cengage Learning.

sore throat. CFS does not have a known cause, but appears to result from a combination of factors.

CFS is the most common name for this disorder, but it also has been called chronic fatigue and immune [dysfunction syndrome] (CFIDS), myalgic encephalomyelitis, low natural killer cell disease, post-viral syndrome, Epstein-Barr disease, and Yuppie flu. CFS has so many names because researchers have been unable to find out exactly what causes it and because there are many similar, overlapping conditions. Reports of a CFS-like syndrome called neurasthenia date back to 1869. Later, people with similar symptoms were said to have fibromyalgia because one of the main symptoms is myalgia, or muscle pain. Because of the similarity of symptoms, fibromyalgia and CFS are considered to be overlapping syndromes.

In the early to mid-1980s, there were outbreaks of CFS in some areas of the United States. Doctors found that many people with CFS had high levels of antibodies to the Epstein-Barr virus (EBV), which causes mononucleosis, in their blood. For a while they thought they had found the culprit, but it turned out that many healthy people also had high EBV antibodies. Scientists have also found high levels of other viral antibodies in the blood of people with CFS. These findings have led many scientists to believe that a virus or combination of viruses may trigger CFS.

CFS was sometimes referred to as Yuppie flu because it seemed to often affect young, middle-class professionals. In fact, CFS can affect people of any gender, age, race, or socioeconomic group. Although anyone can get CFS, most patients diagnosed with CFS are 25–45 years old, and about 80% of cases are in women. Estimates of how many people are afflicted with CFS vary due to the similarity of CFS symptoms to other diseases and the difficulty in identifying it. The Centers for Disease Control and Prevention (CDC) has estimated that four to 10 people per 100,000 in the United States have CFS. According to the

CFIDS Foundation, about 500,000 adults in the United States (0.3% of the population) have CFS. This probably is a low estimate since these figures do not include children and are based on the CDC definition of CFS, which is very strict for research purposes.

Causes and Symptoms

There is no single known cause for CFS. Studies have pointed to several different conditions that might be responsible. These include:

- viral infections
- chemical toxins
- allergies
- immune abnormalities
- psychological disorders

Although the cause is still controversial, many doctors and researchers now think that CFS may not be a single illness. Instead, they think CFS may be a group of symptoms caused by several conditions. One theory is that a microorganism, such as a virus, or a chemical injures the body and damages the immune system, allowing dormant viruses to become active. About 90% of all people have a virus in the herpes family dormant (not actively growing or reproducing) in their bodies since childhood. When these viruses start growing again, the immune system may overreact and produce chemicals called cytokines that can cause flu-like symptoms. Immune abnormalities have been found in studies of people with CFS, although the same abnormalities are also found in people with allergies, autoimmune diseases, cancer, and other disorders.

The role of psychological problems in CFS is very controversial. Because many people with CFS are diagnosed with depression and other psychiatric disorders, some experts conclude that the symptoms of CFS are psychological. However, many people with CFS did not

have psychological disorders before getting the illness. Many doctors think that patients become depressed or anxious because of the effects of the symptoms of their CFS. One recent study concluded that depression was the result of CFS and was not its cause.

Having CFS is not just a matter of being tired. People with CFS have severe fatigue that keeps them from performing their normal daily activities. They find it difficult or impossible to work, attend school, or even to take part in social activities. They may have sleep disturbances that keep them from getting enough rest or they may sleep too much. Many people with CFS feel just as tired after a full night's sleep as before they went to bed. When they exercise or try to be active in spite of their fatigue, people with CFS experience what some patients call "payback"—debilitating exhaustion that can confine them to bed for days.

People with CFS have ongoing fatigue and many other symptoms that can last six months or longer. (© Blend Images/Alamy)

Other symptoms of CFS include:

- muscle pain (myalgia)
- joint pain (arthralgia)
- sore throat
- headache
- fever and chills
- tender lymph nodes
- trouble concentrating
- memory loss

A recent study at the Johns Hopkins University found an abnormality in blood pressure regulation in 22 of 23 patients with CFS. This abnormality, called neurally mediated hypotension, causes a sudden drop in blood pressure when a person has been standing, exercising or exposed to heat for a while. When this occurs, patients feel lightheaded and may faint. They often are exhausted for hours to days after one of these episodes. When treated with salt and medications to stabilize blood pressure, many patients in the study had marked improvements in their CFS symptoms.

Diagnosis

CFS is diagnosed by evaluating symptoms and eliminating other causes of fatigue. Doctors carefully question patients about their symptoms, any other illnesses they have had, and medications they are taking. They also conduct a physical examination, neurological examination, and laboratory tests to identify any underlying disorders or other diseases that cause fatigue. In the United States, many doctors use the CDC case definition to determine whether a patient has CFS.

To be diagnosed with CFS, patients must meet both of the following criteria:

- Unexplained continuing or recurring chronic fatigue for at least six months that is of new or definite onset, is not the result of ongoing exertion, and is not mainly relieved by rest, and causes occupational, educational, social, or personal activities to be greatly reduced.

- Four or more of the following symptoms: loss of short-term memory or ability to concentrate; sore throat; tender lymph nodes; muscle pain; multi-joint pain without swelling or redness; headaches of a new type, pattern, or severity; unrefreshing sleep; and

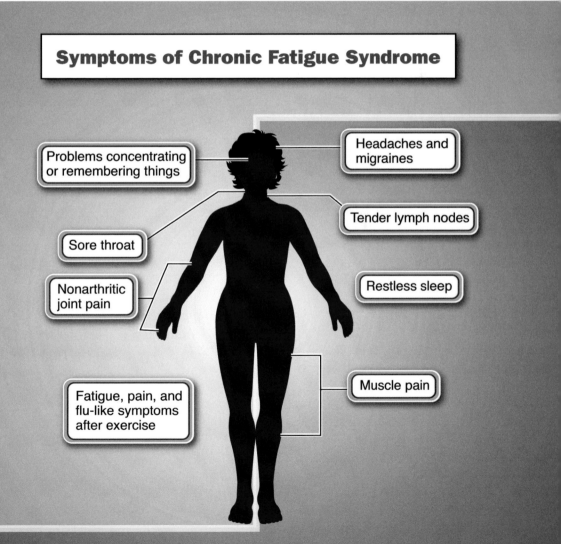

Symptoms of Chronic Fatigue Syndrome

Problems concentrating or remembering things

Headaches and migraines

Sore throat

Tender lymph nodes

Nonarthritic joint pain

Restless sleep

Fatigue, pain, and flu-like symptoms after exercise

Muscle pain

Taken from: *HubPages,* "Is Chronic Fatigue Syndrome Ruining Your Life?," blog entry by Seamist. http://hubpages.com/hub/chronic-fatigue-syndrome-symptoms.

post-exertional malaise (a vague feeling of discomfort or tiredness following exercise or other physical or mental activity) lasting more than 24 hours. These symptoms must have continued or recurred during six or more consecutive months of illness and must not have started before the fatigue began.

Treatment

There is no cure for CFS, but many treatments are available to help relieve the symptoms. Treatments usually are individualized to each person's particular symptoms and needs. The first treatment most doctors recommend is a combination of rest, exercise, and a balanced diet. Prioritizing activities, avoiding overexertion, and resting when needed are key to maintaining existing energy reserves. A program of moderate exercise helps to keep patients from losing physical conditioning, but too much exercise can worsen fatigue and other CFS symptoms. Counseling and stress reduction techniques also may help some people with CFS.

Many medications, nutritional supplements, and herbal preparations have been used to treat CFS. While many of these are unproven, others seem to provide some people with relief. People with CFS should discuss their treatment plan with their doctors and carefully weigh the benefits and risks of each therapy before making a decision.

> ## FAST FACT
>
> According to a 2007 Centers for Disease Control and Prevention media briefing, at least 1 million Americans have CFS, less than 20 percent of whom have been diagnosed. CFS affects four times as many women as men and is most prevalent among adults aged forty to fifty-nine.

Drugs

Nonsteroidal anti-inflammatory drugs (NSAIDs), such as ibuprofen and naproxen, may be used to relieve pain and reduce fever. Another medication that is prescribed to relieve pain and muscle spasms is cyclobenzaprine (sold as Flexeril).

Many doctors prescribe low dosages of antidepressants for their sedative effects and to relieve symptoms of depression. Antianxiety drugs, such as benzodiazepines or buspirone may be prescribed for excessive anxiety that has lasted for at least six months.

Other medications that have been tested or are being tested for treatment of CFS are:

- Fludrocortisone (Florinef), a synthetic steroid, which is currently being tested for treatment of people with CFS. It causes the body to retain salt, thereby increasing blood pressure. It has helped some people with CFS who have neurally mediated hypotension.
- Beta-adrenergic blocking drugs, often prescribed for high blood pressure. Such drugs, including atenolol (Tenoretic, Tenormin) and propranolol (Inderal), are sometimes prescribed for neurally mediated hypotension.
- Gamma globulin, which contains human antibodies to a variety of organisms that cause infection. It has been used experimentally to boost immune function in people with CFS.
- Ampligen, a drug which stimulates the immune system and has antiviral activity. In one small study, ampligen improved mental function in people with CFS.

Alternative Treatments

A variety of nutritional supplements are used for treatment of CFS. Among these are vitamin C, vitamin B_{12}, vitamin A, vitamin E, and various dietary minerals. These supplements may help improve immune and mental functions. Several herbs have been shown to improve immune function and have other beneficial effects. Some that are used for CFS are astragalus (*Astragalus membranaceus*), echinacea (*Echinacea* spp. [species]), garlic (*Allium sativum*), ginseng (*Panax ginseng*), gingko (*Gingko biloba*), evening primrose oil (*Oenothera biennis*), shiitake mushroom extract (*Lentinus edodes*), borage seed oil, and quercetin [a bioflavonoid].

Many people have enhanced their healing process for CFS with the use of a treatment program inclusive of one or more alternative therapies. Stress reduction techniques such as biofeedback, meditation, acupuncture, and yoga may help people with sleep disturbances relax and get more rest. They also help some people reduce depression and anxiety caused by CFS.

Prognosis

The course of CFS varies widely for different people. Some people get progressively worse over time, while others gradually improve. Some individuals have periods of illness that alternate with periods of good health. While many people with CFS never fully regain their health, they find relief from symptoms and adapt to the demands of the disorder by carefully following a treatment plan combining adequate rest, nutrition, exercise, and other therapies.

Because the cause of CFS is not known, there currently are no recommendations for preventing the disorder.

People with Chronic Fatigue Syndrome Need Support

Maria de Lourdes Drachler et al.

Researcher Maria de Lourdes Drachler and colleagues studied the stated views of over twenty-five hundred people with chronic fatigue syndrome (CFS) in order to find out what the sufferers believed they needed. Drachler and her fellow researchers learned that patients wanted to make sense of their symptoms and get a diagnosis, to receive respect and empathy from medical providers, to receive support and understanding from their families and friends, to obtain information about CFS, to adjust their own needs and priorities, to develop ways to manage their limitations, and to maintain or regain social participation. Maria de Lourdes Drachler is a researcher at the School of Allied Health Professionals at the University of East Anglia in England.

We carried out a systematic review of primary research and personal ('own') stories expressing the needs of people with CFS/ME [chronic fatigue syndrome/myalgic encephalomyelitis].... Thirty-two

SOURCE: Maria de Lourdes Drachler et al. "The Expressed Needs of People with Chronic Fatigue Syndrome/Myalgic Encephalomyelitis: A Systematic Review," *BMC Public Health*, vol. 9, 2009. Copyright © 2009 Drachler et al; licensee BioMed Central Ltd. Reproduced by permission.

quantitative and qualitative studies, including the views of over 2500 people with CFS/ME with mainly moderate or severe illness severity, met the inclusion criteria. The following major support needs emerged: 1) The need to make sense of symptoms and gain diagnosis, 2) for respect and empathy from service providers, 3) for positive attitudes and support from family and friends, 4) for information on CFS/ME, 5) to adjust views and priorities, 6) to develop strategies to manage impairments and activity limitations, and 7) to develop strategies to maintain/regain social participation. . . .

The Need to Make Sense of Symptoms and Gain Diagnosis

Making sense of CFS/ME symptoms and gaining a diagnosis were crucial as many did not immediately recognise CFS/ME in themselves, and their symptoms were not understood by health professionals, family or friends: "*So many parts of my body were malfunctioning*", but I had "*no idea what was wrong*", which was very frightening.

Not having a diagnosis posed challenges for relationships with friends, colleagues and relatives. People struggled to make decisions about which people could be given how much, and what type, of information about their health, selecting symptoms that appeared to have greater legitimacy. They worried that it would not seem credible to blame fatigue before a diagnosis was established. This sense of living with a mystery illness, lacking legitimacy, further compromised participation in many areas, such as family, work, leisure, health and social care.

Although diagnosis was perceived as crucial, the search for a diagnosis in adults and young people could take a long time—for some it involved more than ten years of consulting health professionals without being taken seriously, or entailed long journeys—"*nearly 1000 miles to get to a doctor who could diagnose me.*" Some reported that doctors seemed not to believe in the existence of CFS/ME. To *"come to terms with the mystery illness and to get a diagnosis was hard enough"* and made them feel ill, frightened, angry and alone, bereft of support.

A diagnosis gave a name to their condition, opening a gateway for communicating needs, accessing support services and learning about their illness. Once the diagnosis was confirmed, some experienced a tremendous sense of relief, even though at the time they did not know what the diagnosis meant. Although important, the diagnosis was also seen as bringing problems as *"learning that there is no explanation for a terrifying condition (known as CFS/ME) is devastating psychologically and socially."*

The Need for Respect and Empathy from Service Providers

Recognition of expressed needs by service providers was perceived as crucial to align perspectives and receive care needed to manage and gain control over their lives.

A technician runs tests on blood samples from CFS patients to rule out other disorders. Some sufferers have seen doctors for ten years before finally being correctly diagnosed. **(Will & Deni McIntyre/Time Life Pictures/Getty Images)**

People with CFS/ME emphasised the need for recognition that CFS/ME is a multi-faceted, disabling illness. Many reported that living with CFS/ME was particularly hard when doctors disbelieved in the illness, when CFS/ME was assumed to be a psychological illness, the

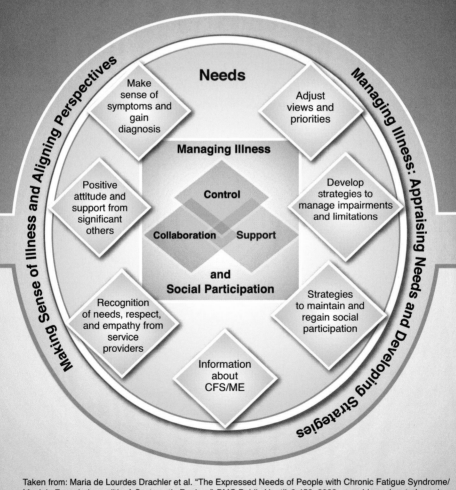

Self-Expressed Needs of People with CFS and Myalgic Encephalomyelitis (CFS/ME)

Taken from: Maria de Lourdes Drachler et al. "The Expressed Needs of People with Chronic Fatigue Syndrome/Myalgic Encephalomyelitis: A Systematic Review," *BMC Public Heatlh* 9:458, 2009. www.biomedcentral.com/1471-2458/9/458.

breadth of symptoms and their impact were not fully acknowledged and/or were attributed to depression, psychosomatic conditions or malingering. In such situations they perceived themselves to be seen as 'hypochondriac', 'malingerers' or 'troublemaking'.

Disbelief and lack of empathy by health care providers emerged as common experiences and carried the threat of receiving only psychological treatment or not having their needs recognised as legitimate. This appeared to further compromise access to health and social care, and frequently led to a cycle of chaos. Many reported leaving a doctor's office in tears, knowing that they were very sick, but having no way to convince others about the legitimacy of their illness. Even in cases of severe pain or disability, people were told there was nothing wrong with them, *". . . and if I couldn't walk, it was psychological."* Others were told that recovery was a matter of getting up and pulling themselves together. *"I'll tell you what was said to me. . . . 'Put your make up on, have your hair done and you'll feel a lot better.' . . . I found it quite insulting."* People with CFS/ME felt that the battles they needed to fight for support made their lives more difficult: *"I think the plights of people with ME, the difficulties that are sort of added through the fights with [the] benefit system and the health service."* *"For the patient the process [of claiming long term disability benefits] is humiliating, exhausting and at times, results in a lengthier and more severe period of disablement."*

The Need to Be Treated as a Whole Person

The need to be treated as a whole person with a body, mind and spirit was another frequently unmet need. The lack of recognition of this need was especially serious for the severely ill, where their condition constrained their ability to communicate and take control of the management of their illness. People reported being *"treated like a non-person"*. One woman, bed-bound for twenty five years with hypersensitivity to various stimuli, was not recognised as rational or aware: *"'Your wife's a vegetable' one helpful doctor shouted on the phone as Jesse [her husband] sat next to me six inches from my ear. It wasn't at all true. . . . But on the outside, I could have been mistaken for a head of broccoli. I was almost completely locked in."*

Lack of respect for, or belief in, people's self expression of health needs, was a major problem for those who were severely affected, disadvantaged or from minority groups. For example, a woman with terrible abdominal pain was not taken as a medical emergency with legitimate call on resource: *"Why was I having to act as my own medical spokesperson? What if I were too weak to talk? What if I were intimidated by the hospital because I was less well educated, or poor, or black in a sea of non-black higher authority, or English was my second language? Who would be my advocate then?"* This lack of control affected health seeking behaviour. . . .

Although most reported experiences within the health and social services were negative, some people described examples of good practice. Health professionals conveyed messages of empathy, encouragement and personal commitment: by giving information and feedback, by demonstrating expertise about CFS/ME or a genuine interest in learning about it; by listening to, and discussing, available treatments; by encouraging the client to ask questions, not to suffer in silence; and help others, like teachers, understand this illness; and by informing where and how to find adequate care. Clinical psychologists and other health professionals were valued in providing psychological support to deal with this life-disrupting condition and the stigma associated with CFS/ME: *"the clinical psychologist who helped me begin to trust in myself again."* Also important was demonstrating sympathy with the client's situation: *"[The doctor] just sat and looked at me with such compassion and empathy—I could have hugged him."*

The Need for Positive Attitudes and Support from Family and Friends

Support and understanding from family and friends was considered vital, and lack of social support was identified as a perpetuating factor of fatigue severity and functional impairment. However, social isolation is often associated with CFS/ME. One young person commented, *"The worst thing was not having any friends; it's important to have support from people who like you and give you confidence."* The attitudes of significant others were crucial for young people: *"I think the single most helpful thing of all is when people don't judge . . ."* and adults, *"My husband has been a tower of strength and he understands, he's never questioned, he's never said . . . you'll feel better soon. He understands and that has been very supportive."*

Although health professionals were expected to facilitate positive attitudes of family and friends, some doctors caused others to dismiss symptoms leading to lack of support from family: *"When my husband comes home from work, he always says, 'Why are you sleeping all the time? The doctor says there is nothing wrong. . . .'"* The disbelief of significant others left them feeling bereft of support, frustrated and fearful.

The Need for Information Relating to CFS/ME

Both before and after a CFS/ME diagnosis was established, information about the condition appeared central in allowing people to gain control of their lives. Some reported that medical knowledge acquired through friends' searches and emotional support helped them break a cycle of social withdrawal and disapproval, whilst others offered doctors their own diagnosis. Discussions with, and feedback from, doctors during diagnosis helped people make sense of, and manage, their illness.

While diagnosis allowed access to formal support services, it was often difficult to find accessible services with up-to-date knowledge of CFS/ME and where professionals were sympathetic. Knowledge about CFS/ME, alongside support from significant others and empathy from health professionals, empowered people to get the care they needed. Health professionals conveyed useful information when listening and discussing available treatments and by providing information about where and how to find adequate care.

Equally important for many was information about, and help with, financial support. This need was vividly expressed, since for many *"their finances were severely strained"* due to reduced job opportunities for themselves or their family carers and additional costs of support. Financial limitations in turn further limited social participation (as many social activities are expensive). While people with CFS/ME often felt forced to apply for disability benefits, they were not always able to demonstrate their eligibility.

ME support groups and associations were mentioned as valuable sources of information and contact with other people with CFS/ME to help in grasping the *"strange, disabling but unpredictable nature of this condition."* However, some had chosen not to take part in support as they could not find the energy to participate or because *"identifying themselves and other people with CFS/ME primarily as people suffering from an illness"* would be detrimental to their positive thinking. . . .

The Need to Adjust Views and Priorities

Approaches to managing impairments ranged from trying almost anything in desperation, including pharmaceuticals, complementary medicine and diets, while some younger people allowed CFS/ME to run its natural course. To come to terms with their illness and work towards wellness, many pointed out that they had to learn to recognize and address their whole self as a physical, emotional and spiritual being, as no one type of treatment could provide all the answers. *"No amount of knowledge can help someone to make the necessary internal adjustments; that has to do with attitude."* Changes called for adjustments in self-valuation and attitudes, increasing awareness of limitations, decreasing focus on achievements such as school grades, refocusing and re-prioritising relationships and health. This acceptance was often described as very difficult: *"It's been a very hard slog mentally to accept what I've got."*

Accepting and learning to deal with limitations and changing lives could impose great challenges, which appeared to vary greatly between individuals and in differing periods of the condition. Disruption ranged from being able to maintain activities of daily living, employment, education and communication only at the cost of much effort and compromise in participative activities, to catastrophic limitations, as people found themselves in a wheelchair, housebound or bedbound. One man reported that *". . . for someone who had been a self-sufficient, tax-paying, highly motivated individual all my life, having to now accept disability (which is also a humiliation, as I do not feel that I am earning it as I did when I was well) was a great challenge."* A first-hand account reports: *"I couldn't read talk, listen, look, visit, or get up from a supine position. I had to wear a light-blocking mask over my eyes in a darkened room at all times. Nurses had to feed me. They had to whisper if and when they talked to me."* Such limitations were closely related to restrictions on participation in relationships and personal expression. This was experienced as frightening, since well-being depended on carers to identify and respect their needs.

Accepting help and equipment, such as use of a dishwasher, a walking stick or employing a [house]cleaner

> ## FAST FACT
>
> The annual total value of lost productivity in the United States due to chronic fatigue syndrome is $9.1 billion, according to a 2004 study by the Centers for Disease Control and Prevention. This represents, on average, about half of the household and labor force productivity of the average person with CFS.

could therefore also pose a challenge. For others, befriending services, advocacy and learning self-advocacy as part of independent living training proved helpful. As equipment and others' help could be seen as a badge of disability, they could pose difficulties for self-image and sense of independence despite being practically useful. *"I found it difficult to admit to myself that I needed help, and even more difficult to ask for it."* The same woman described hiding a fold-up walking stick in a bag as *"such was my pride I tried desperately hard not to use it."*

Accepting psychological support appeared to help some people deal with the stressful experience of living with CFS/ME, however, others saw accepting psychotherapy as implying that they had a psychological problem rather than a physical illness.

The Need to Develop Strategies to Manage Impairments and Activity Limitations

Many people with CFS/ME found themselves in a constant balancing act over how best to use their limited energy resources: *"The secret of coping is to accept that the imbalance exists, to weigh up the resources and to make a choice about how to use them."* One study emphasized [that] *"when energy is severely limited there is little time to spare for others and virtually none for outside the family."* This prioritisation may preclude access to forms of support such as CFS/ME self-help groups.

On occasions *"even sitting up in bed could become too difficult"* and a small increase in physical or mental activity could cause relapse *"with a vengeance."* Rest and activity reduction could bring symptom relief, but was experienced as challenging and difficult to achieve and often only brought temporary relief. Planned rest periods were important for many, including this young person: *"Sometimes I don't feel I need to rest, but I still rest because in the past I haven't felt I needed to rest, but then the next day I was really tired and it took longer for that to go."*

Finding meaningful occupation within the confines of the illness was important. *"I certainly couldn't do anything like knitting. I couldn't concentrate on a pattern. . . . Eventually, I thought I'm fed up with just sitting watching television doing nothing, so I took up tapestry."* Adjustments were made by routinely appraising how successful their coping initiatives had been, in the context of self-knowledge and the perspectives of significant others. One person with CFS/ME reported having tried *"to do something every single day, like, otherwise [the illness] just walks all over me."*

While activity-rest balance is important, it needs preparation and recovery time, making planning complex. Overdoing exercise was *"terrible, it makes me feel really ill"*, but gentle exercises to re-build muscles was helpful for some. For some young people, pacing activities, and gradually increasing activity, was useful when not linked to achievement pressure or over-riding good judgment about when to stop and rest. *"Don't do too much but set yourself targets. I didn't like being pushed and hated the idea of walking everyday, but it worked."*

The Need to Develop Strategies to Maintain/Regain Social Participation

Impairments and activity limitations affected people's ability to maintain previous roles: *"You go through the grieving thing; it's the death of a whole lifestyle."* Losses of multiple aspects of social participation seemed so painful that some people made huge efforts to maintain their informal social life, work and educational role. Leisure was an important need, often sacrificed to enable participation in employment and education, or as a direct consequence of impairments, economic disadvantage and social isolation. As relationships changed with friends, family and work, dealing with separation from former lives meant having to reassess and prioritise those relationships which were most supportive.

Outside the family, education was the major focus of social participation for many young people. Rarely attending school, some reported having lost connection with friends and teachers. Home tuition [study], a common alternative, allowed a flexible schedule of learning within the limits of their condition, but reduced social participation at an important stage of social development. Although intensive work required by school activities worsened the health of some children, others could ignore this effect, at least in the short term: *"I may think I am going to go into school so I may as well try and feel well."* For other young people, school meant not having their needs acknowledged, being discriminated against and bullied by peers and educational workers who did not understand the complexity of their illness, considered them malingerers or lazy. School for children, and jobs for adults, were signifiers of living 'normally', providing purposeful activity, an opportunity for social interaction, a sense of achievement, self-value and social recognition, income and social security.

However, needs stemming from work and education were substantial, posing difficult choices. Pacing work, by resting when fatigued, often meant taking work home to get it completed, and stressful decisions had to be made about disclosure; expectations of stigma made some conceal their illness. However, in a supportive environment, careful disclosure seemed helpful: *"They were very good and arranged a room with a bed in [it] for me. . . . So I used to nap between lectures, that was the only way that I could get through the day."*

In the absence of adequate social support, the effort of maintaining employment raised stress, compromised family roles and leisure activities or exacerbated the illness. Decisions therefore had to be made about whom to disclose to, the extent of disclosure, and how far to limit activities. Others, severely affected by impairments, were discharged from their jobs when people learnt about their illness, or could not cope with working demands—some *"broke down crying . . . as they described what they had had to give up. . . . For many that meant their jobs."* Consequences included loss of earnings and radical life-style changes such as moving home [with parents] as income reduced.

Others lost access to recommended treatments as they could no longer pay.

Many psychological and physical demands can be made on people with CFS/ME and . . . major needs may be largely unmet due to poor recognition of CFS/ME as an illness or of its impact. The review has shown that the lack of recognition of needs and poor support from the health and social systems further compromise socioeconomic status, activities of daily living, social participation and personal development, thereby exacerbating the impact of the illness in their lives.

The Prevalence of Chronic Fatigue Syndrome Is Difficult to Determine

Peter D. White

In the following viewpoint Peter D. White says that, while physicians care more about the symptoms of patients they see than about the prevalence of an illness in the general population, it is still important to know how common a condition is in order to set public health-care priorities. Thus, defining criteria must be adopted. In the case of chronic fatigue syndrome (CFS) this is difficult to determine, since definitions of the condition vary, and there is no biological marker for it. The results of CFS surveys vary, and the most recent has found its prevalence to be up to ten times greater than the results of previous surveys. However, methodology can also vary, as it does in the surveys White discusses. Furthermore, many people were found who suffered from chronic fatigue but did not meet all the criteria for a diagnosis of CFS. In the author's opinion, those criteria are arbitrary and should be broadened. White is a professor of psychological medicine at the Wolfson Institute of Preventive Medicine, Barts, and the London School of Medicine and Dentistry in London, England.

SOURCE: Peter D. White, "How Common Is Chronic Fatigue Syndrome; How Long Is a Piece Of String?," *Population Health Metrics*, June 8, 2007. Copyright © 2007 White; licensee BioMed Central Ltd. Reproduced by permission.

One of the most difficult tasks in medicine is to accurately measure how common illnesses are. Why do we do it? Justifications include being able to plan health care and public health priorities, as well as highlighting specific diseases for extra funding for both health care and research. Yet the jobbing physician [one who works temporarily at different places] at the sharp edge of clinical practice cares little about the exact prevalence of a disease or illness, since this is all too obvious from the frequency of the problems presented by patients who come through the door.

How Do You Measure a Syndrome?

If the disease in question has no biological marker and is difficult to define clinically, the problem of working out the accurate prevalence becomes esoteric [mysterious]. Chronic fatigue syndrome (CFS) is just such an illness. It has as many synonyms as putative causes, being also called myalgic encephalomyelitis, chronic immune dysfunction syndrome, and post-viral fatigue syndrome, amongst others. Since fatigue is one of the most common symptoms reported by patients in general, delineating a specific syndrome with fatigue as a central feature risks arbitrary decisions about ascertainment. Do we categorise the syndrome on the basis of the severity of fatigue, the number of associated symptoms, or the severity of the resultant disability? Even measuring the consequent disability gives us problems since there are only weak correlations between subjective and objective observations. It is therefore no great surprise that half of all doctors do not even believe it exists.

And yet, patients and their organisations constantly criticize doctors both for not believing in the existence of CFS and for not taking patients seriously. Even politicians seem to take the problem more seriously than some doctors do. This may be as much to do with successful lobbying as the economic costs of CFS, which have been estimated as $9 billion per annum just for lost productivity in the USA. Doctors don't understand things they can't see or measure, and patients mistrust doctors who don't understand them. We are in a conundrum.

One Way Forward

The Centers for Disease Control and Prevention (CDC) in the United States of America are one of the few health care agencies who do take CFS seriously, to the extent of supporting a $4 million public education campaign, which started last year [2006]. They have also led the way in providing operationalised criteria in order to standardize the diagnosis of CFS. Their latest research programme has been based on a large survey of the adult (18–59 years old) population of the state of Georgia, USA, in order to better understand the epidemiology and etiology of CFS. Their previous study of prevalence, in Wichita, Kansas, suggested a prevalence of 0.24%. Another independent population survey in Chicago suggested a prevalence of 0.42%. The CDC has now repeated and extended the Wichita study in Georgia, and found a prevalence of between six and ten times greater, with 2.5% of the population suffering from CFS. If this prevalence was both accurate and representative of the USA as a whole, this would suggest that some 7.5 million Americans were sufferers, compared to the previous estimates of 0.7 to 1.2 million.

> **FAST FACT**
>
> According to the Chronic Fatigue and Immune Dysfunction Syndrome (CFIDS) Association of America, more than 80 percent of those who have CFIDS are undiagnosed.

A Cautious Interpretation

Could this really be true? The authors are sensibly cautious in their interpretations, and point out the uncertainties inherent within the study. There are three main reasons why we should be cautious about interpretation and generalizing from this finding. Compared to previous studies, there were important differences in the method of ascer-

William Reeves, former head of the CDC's Chronic Fatigue Syndrome Research Program, gives an interview about the program's work. (AP Images/John Bazemore)

tainment used in the Georgia study that may help to explain the greater prevalence. Most importantly, the Georgia study used a different initial screening question. Instead of asking whether a household member was suffering from "fatigue", as previously done, the screening question asked about being "unwell", by which was meant having one or more of the following symptoms for a month or more: "fatigue, cognitive impairment, unrefreshing sleep, muscle pain, joint pain, sore throat, tender lymph nodes, or headache" (all being likely symptoms of CFS). The authors suggested that this stratagem picked up an extra 11.5% of CFS cases. A strength of the Georgia survey was the use of standardised measures of symptoms and disability. However in order to count someone as fatigued—the central criterion for a diagnosis of CFS—individuals only needed to score the median or more of the well population, either for fatigue or inactivity. In a previous study, the same authors found that using such standardised measures picked up three times as many cases of CFS than verbatim enquiries.

These methodological differences mean it is not possible to directly compare the prevalence of CFS in Georgia with previous studies.

Comorbid [accompanying] psychiatric conditions may have inflated the prevalence. A previous study found an equally high point prevalence of CFS (2.6%), by surveying United Kingdom primary care patients. However, when those patients who also had a comorbid psychiatric disorder were excluded, the prevalence fell to 0.5%. Although it will be important to publish the prevalence of comorbid psychiatric disorders in the Georgian survey, the argument can still be put that these comorbid

Conditions That Exclude a Diagnosis of CFS

- Any active medical condition that may explain the presence of chronic fatigue, such as untreated hypothyroidism, sleep apnea and narcolepsy, or side effects of medication

- A past illness that may not have been completely resolved with treatment, such as some types of malignancies and chronic cases of hepatitis

- Any past or current diagnosis of a major psychiatric disorder

- Alcohol or other substance abuse

- Severe obesity

Taken from: Centers for Disease Control and Prevention, *Chronic Fatigue Syndrome*: "The 1994 Case Definition" (abridged version). www.cdc.gov/cfs/general/case_definition/abridged.html.

psychiatric disorders were secondary to having chronic ill-health, rather than the primary and explanatory condition. The current design cannot determine the direction of causality, although previous longitudinal studies suggest that psychiatric ill health can both follow and precede CFS.

Georgia may not be representative of the USA as a whole. For instance, we do not know the body mass index (BMI) of the Georgian sample. The Wichita sample of CFS cases contained 43% of subjects with a BMI of 30 or over, representing significant obesity. This compares with 20% in the USA as a whole. Since obesity is associated with fatigue, a similar proportion in Georgia might inflate the prevalence of CFS.

What can we conclude from this very large survey? Although methodological issues may help to explain the high prevalence of CFS found in this study, the argument can still be made that the prevalence of CFS is greater than previously thought. CFS is at least as common in ethnic minorities in the USA as in the ethnic Caucasian majority; a welcome replication of previous studies. CFS is not an exclusively white syndrome. Social issues may help to explain why women suffer CFS more than men. But perhaps the most important conclusion is that there were about twice as many people in Georgia who were unwell with fatigue, who did not meet the criteria for CFS. Our current criteria for diagnosing CFS are arbitrary, and we need to widen the net to capture all those people who become so chronically tired and unwell that they can't live their lives to their full potential. The jobbing physician does not close the door on those who don't meet criteria.

Myalgic Encephalomyelitis and CFS Are Not the Same

National Alliance for Myalgic Encephalomyelitis

The National Alliance for Myalgic Encephalomyelitis is privately funded by patients with a desire to clearly delineate this neuroimmune disease, with the goal of finding effective treatments and a cure. Although myalgic encephalomyelitis (ME) and chronic fatigue syndrome (CFS) are generally considered to be different names for the same illness, some doctors believe there is a distinction between them. The alliance holds that confusion exists because of government bureaucracy and politics that result in the opinions of researchers being ignored. Almost all patients with ME fit the diagnostic criteria for CFS, the alliance says, but the reverse is not true. To have ME, a patient must have central nervous system abnormalities that can be measured by neurological tests such as brain scans. The case definition for CFS does not require this procedure, and people have been diagnosed with CFS who turned out to have treatable medical conditions.

SOURCE: National Alliance for Myalgic Encephalomyelitis, "M.E. or CFS: Clearing Up the Confusion," NAME-US.org, 2009. Reproduced by permission.

Confusion and controversy abound as to whether ME and CFS are the same entity. Unfortunately, government bureaucracy and politics have had too much to do with perpetuating this confusion, ignoring and even ridiculing expert advice from clinicians and researchers in the field who have seen patients with this disease daily for years. . . .

With the recent discovery of the retrovirus, XMRV, in most ME/CFS patients, using both ME and CFS definitions, and with research accelerating and ongoing, we are not certain at this time whether the newly named disease entity, XAND (XMRV Associated Neuroimmune Disease) will encompass ME, CFS and other neuroimmune diseases once-and-for-all. Time will tell. We hope, as this exciting new research progresses, that *all* ME and CFS patients are soon rid of confusion and stigma associated with these labels.

As Dr. David Bell, veteran ME/CFS clinician and researcher, stated, "And while I am making rash predictions, let's talk about the name of this illness. It has been a favorite topic of mine since [the publication of my book] *The Disease of a Thousand Names*. Chronic fatigue syndrome is miserable name. I think that XMRV is going to turn out to be the puppet-master that pulls the strings of illnesses variously called CFS, ME, fibromyalgia, atypical multiple sclerosis, chronic mononucleosis. . . . And if it does, the name should be XAND, for Xmrv Associated Neuroimmune Disease. I heard Mrs. Annette Whittemore [president of the Whittemore Peterson Institute for Neuro-Immune Disease] use this term and it feels right. History."

"Where the one essential characteristic of ME is acquired CNS [central nervous system] dysfunction, that of CFS is primarily chronic fatigue."

Dr. Byron Hyde of the Nightingale Research Foundation makes the above very simple yet profound statement in his essay, "The Complexities of Diagnosis" (Chapter 3 in

Illnesses Similar to CFS

These illnesses all have similar symptoms, such as fatigue, muscle and/or joint pain, disturbed and/or unrefreshing sleep, headaches, memory problems, difficulty concentrating, depression, and others. Some doctors believe these illnesses are different types of the same syndrome.

Chronic fatigue syndrome (CFS)	Cause unknown—involves much more than fatigue
Myalgic encephalomyelitis (ME)	Another name for CFS—sometimes considered the same
Fibromyalgia syndrome (FMS)	Cause unknown—characterized by painful trigger points
Post-traumatic stress disorder (PTSD)	Caused by anxiety following a traumatic experience
Gulf War syndrome (GWS)	Affects veterans and others exposed to chemical weapons
Multiple chemical sensitivity (MCS)	Not recognized by the American Medical Association
Lyme disease	Caused by bacteria from a tick bite
Chronic Epstein-Barr disease	Caused by a virus—a former name for CFS
Major depressive disorder (MDD)	A psychiatric illness that often has physical symptoms

[Compiled by editor.]

Handbook of Chronic Fatigue Syndrome). While just about all patients with ME will fit the definition for CFS, not all of those with CFS will fit the definition for ME. (But technically, the CDC [Centers for Disease Control and Prevention's] CFS definition excludes those patients with other serious illnesses that include fatigue as a symptom. Therefore a patient formally diagnosed with ME, a serious neurological illness of CNS dysfunction—debilitating fatigue being merely one of *many* disabling symptoms—would be ruled out of the CFS definition. If a patient does not fit the definition for ME and is given a diagnosis of CFS without further investigation into the cause of the symptoms, it would be tragic if a treatable illness was missed. And this has happened on numerous occasions.

ME and CFS are described by some as a "medically explained" illness with no biomarkers. Do not accept this; it is far from the truth. The research cited on our Research pages and others websites, as well as specialized and more in-depth testing as suggested in the [Canadian] Consensus Document and in the Nightingale Definition, explain many of the symptoms ME and CFS-labeled patients suffer—tests that, when interpreted together, can give the patient and doctor a more complete picture of what's going on in patients' bodies. It may also help differentiate whether the patient has ME, or chronic fatigue arising from some other serious illness that may be treatable.

Descriptions Are as Individual as the Patient

There are as many descriptions of this disease as there are patients, because symptom prominence varies from patient to patient. But they all will have a common theme: crushing exhaustion that never goes away, no matter how much you rest; that the simplest things most people take for granted physically and mentally now seem like insurmountable tasks. For example, taking out the trash has become like a march up a mountain, or deciding what you need at the grocery store makes your brain swirl like a page-long physics equation. And once you have tackled one or two of those chores, you feel an overwhelming compulsion to lie down and rest, even though you know it will do little good. And usually there is widespread muscle pain that seems to radiate right out of the spine and into the muscles throughout some or all parts of the body.

A severe hangover that never goes away, that varies in intensity day-to-day, even hour-to-hour, is how ME and CFS are often described, or "the flu that never goes away," year after year. Add to that many of the symptoms—some coming and going or waxing and waning, others ever-present, always aggravated by tasks you used to give barely a passing thought to—and you have a person in a state of debility that has been compared by researchers and clinicians to MS [multiple sclerosis], cancer and AIDS.

FAST FACT

Although ME/CFS is not generally considered fatal, it occasionally appears as the cause of death on death certificates; in exceptional cases it has resulted in heart or other organ damage. There have also been cases in which it led to suicide.

Many scientists would describe ME or CFS in less personal, more technical terms. Words like "post-exertional malaise" and "neurocognitive impairment" sound fairly important, but simply do not convey what the patient is really experiencing. But the clinicians and researchers who have collectively worked with thousands of ME and CFS-labeled patients know that "there is no word in the the English lexicon that describes the lack of stamina, the paucity of energy, the absolute malaise and turpitude that accompanies this illness." (Dr. Charles Lapp)

Then What Is the Difference Between ME and CFS?

ME experts from the U.K., U.S., Canada, Australia and many other countries who have studied this disease have stated that it's the definitions that determine the diagnosis. The current Consensus Document and most ME definitions . . . require the major criteria of severe muscle fatigue following minimal exertion with prolonged recovery time, and neurological disturbances, especially autonomic, cognitive and sensory functions, and variable involvement of cardiac and other systems, with a prolonged relapsing course. This is a very specific list of criteria, and a major point to note is that the CNS (central nervous system) dysfunction of ME can be measured.

A woman undergoes a tilt table procedure to determine whether her blackouts are caused by neurally mediated hypotension (NMH), an abnormality of blood pressure regulation that is common in ME/CFS patients and may be helped by medication. Patients who have NMH may experience loss of consciousness after being tilted from a lying to a standing position. **(David Parker/Photo Researchers, Inc.)**

Alternatively, CFS definitions present the major criterion of fatigue that lasts 6 months and reduces the level of function by at least 50%. Post-exertional malaise and neurological abnormalities are considered minor and optional criteria. So this broad definition could encompass any of many illnesses in which fatigue plays a role. Fatigue is not only a symptom of numerous illnesses, but it is something experienced by normal, healthy people. And there are no reliable objective ways to measure fatigue.

"The primary diagnostic criterion for ME is acquired CNS change. We have excellent tools for measuring these physiological and neuropsychological changes: SPECT [a brain scanning technology for evaluating disorders of the central nervous system] xenon SPECT, PET [positron emission tomography] and neuropsychological testing. CFS patients may not have any of these findings." . . .

Dr. Byron Hyde, author of the Nightingale Definition of ME states, "I do not describe a patient as having ME unless there is an abnormal SPECT. If the SPECT is normal, I often repeat it along with xenon SPECT. If the brain scans remain normal, I conclude that it is unlikely to be ME I then refer to the patient as a CFS patient and search for other causes of the fatigue syndrome."

Dr. Hyde has described patients that have come to him with a "CFS" or psychiatric diagnosis that he has investigated more thoroughly. Some he has diagnosed with ME after thorough interview, including determining acute or gradual onset, neurological, cardiac and other screening. But in many others he has found underlying, treatable causes for their debilitating fatigue. Some examples he gives are:

1) One man came to him diagnosed as a psychiatric patient which Dr. Hyde initially agreed with, due to the man's obvious irrational behavior during Dr. Hyde's interview with him. The man said he slept a lot, was still tired after sleeping and felt he had "chronic fatigue syndrome," since he met the CDC CFS case definition criteria. Dr. Hyde simply listened to the man and observed his behavior over the course of two hours. He gave the man a requisition for a few tests which within days revealed he was severely diabetic with extreme hyperlipidemia (high cholesterol/triglycerides, etc.). Within weeks of beginning treatment, the man was behaving rationally, and it was further determined he had had a recent myocardial infarction (heart attack).

2) A woman from the U.S. who had been diagnosed with "CFS" by several ME/CFS physicians came to Dr. Hyde with significant brain dysfunction and overwhelming fatigue. He had Doppler tests done on her the same day that found "80% obstruction of both internal carotids [arteries] and complete obstruction of the basilar artery feeding the brain." Internists, neurologists and ME/CFS specialists in the U.S. had all missed the obvious. "The obstruction in one of the arteries was removed and she improved."

[Dr. Hyde] . . . and others state that doctors should also take a complete patient history to determine other significant factors that distinguish ME from CFS and other fatiguing illnesses.

CHAPTER 2

Controversies Concerning Chronic Fatigue Syndrome

A Virus May Cause Chronic Fatigue Syndrome

Sam Kean

In 2009 scientists made a discovery that they believed might identify the cause of chronic fatigue syndrome (CFS). They found traces of a virus called XMRV in the blood cells of two-thirds of their sample of CFS patients, compared with only one-twenty-fifth in people who were healthy. According to writer Sam Kean, other scientists questioned the validity of the experiment and did experiments of their own, which did not produce the same result. Many scientists have suggested that CFS is a group of symptoms that can have various causes; in some cases the XMRV virus and in others, something else. It is also possible that there may be different strains of the virus in different parts of the world. Kean is a science writer based in Washington, DC.

Here we go again. Late last year [2009], scientists seemed to be homing in on the cause of chronic fatigue syndrome (CFS)—excessive tiredness and other symptoms that have no known biological cause—by finding a supposed viral link. But a new paper

Photo on facing page. A doctor leads CFS patients in a discussion group. Controversy surrounds CFS, as many patients believe the current name does not convey the seriousness of the problems for those afflicted. (Robert Lahser/MCT/Landov)

SOURCE: Sam Kean, "Chronic Fatigue Syndrome Attacked Again," *ScienceNOW*, January 6, 2010. Reproduced by permission.

challenges that link, a development that may plunge the field back into the same confusion and acrimony that has characterized it for years.

Many CFS patients report that their symptoms began after an acute viral infection. Yet scientists have been unable to pin CFS on common viruses such as the Epstein-Barr virus. As a result, patients have faced skepticism for years that CFS might not be a real disease, or that it is perhaps a psychiatric disorder.

A team of American researchers thought it finally struck pay dirt last October when it reported in *Science* that it found DNA traces of a virus in the blood cells of two-thirds of 101 patients with CFS, compared with 4% of 218 healthy controls. XMRV is a rodent retrovirus also implicated in an aggressive prostate cancer, though why it might cause or be associated with CFS remains unclear.

Other scientists were dubious about the XMRV connection. They criticized the Americans for not explaining enough about the demographics of their patients and the procedures to control for contamination. Several virologists around the world practically sprinted to their labs to redo the experiments, and the discovery that a clinic associated with the *Science* paper was selling a $650 diagnostic test for XMRV made the issue more pressing. A British team already exploring the XMRV-prostate cancer link won the race, submitting a paper to debunk the claim on 1 December.

The team, led by Myra McClure, a professor of retrovirology at Imperial College London, examined DNA from the blood of 186 CFS patients ranging in age from 19 to 70, with an average age of 40. Most were markedly unwell. McClure's team used a PCR machine—which copies and amplifies scraps of DNA—to search for two viral sequences, one from XMRV and the other from a closely related

FAST FACT

Even if XMRV is found in most people with chronic fatigue syndrome, it cannot be the single cause of the disorder because the virus is also found in some people who are healthy. This means that at least one other factor must contribute to CFS.

virus. They discovered nothing. At a press conference discussing the results, published in *PLoS ONE*, McClure was blunt and confident: "If there was one copy of the virus in those samples, we would have detected it."

This null result prompts the question of what—if anything—was wrong with the original paper. In their own paper, the *PLoS ONE* authors seem to suggest that contamination was at fault, stating that they were careful to work in labs that had never handled XMRV and in PCR machines that analyze no mouse tissues. But McClure says her group merely wanted to make that explicit, not accuse anyone.

Regardless, the American team followed the same procedures, says Vincent Lombardi, a biochemist at the

A technician works with blood samples from CFS patients. A virus has been identified in many CFS patients' blood, but it has not been determined to be a cause of the disorder. (AP Images/John Bazemore)

Whittemore Peterson Institute for Neuro-Immune Disease in Reno, Nevada, and co-author of the *Science* paper. He also expressed bewilderment that the McClure group didn't search its CFS samples for the same DNA sequence as his team had, raising the possibility that that's why the two groups came up with different results. McClure and colleagues, however, looked for not only an XMRV sequence but also a sequence in a closely related virus, MLV. That MLV sequence, highly conserved among viruses of its class, would presumably have been found if XMRV was present, they said.

XMRV May Be Hard to Detect

One distinct possibility, says John Coffin, a microbiologist at Tufts University in Medford, Massachusetts, who studies retroviruses, is that both papers are right. He called the *PLoS ONE* paper too "preliminary" to settle the debate and said XMRV could show more genetic variety, and thus be harder to detect, than anyone assumed. It's also possible that distinct strains of XMRV appear in different parts of the world, like the retroviruses HIV and HTLV (a leukemia virus).

Coffin says one more possibility, raised by many different scientists, is that CFS is actually a suite of diseases that presents the same symptoms and so might have many causes. Lombardi seconds this point. "It's naïve to think that everyone with chronic fatigue has the same etiology. There's probably going to be a subset of people with CFS that have XMRV, and it will probably end up being classified as XMRV-related CFS."

All of this leaves doctors and patients in a muddle. There's no doubt they're hungry for information. Out of curiosity, Lombardi did a Google search on "XMRV" the day before the *Science* paper hit and found about 22,500 hits. Three months later, there are 400,000 hits.

But some scientists, including Coffin and McClure, fear that Lombardi's clinic took advantage of that hun-

Retroviruses Known to Infect Humans

Virus	Year Discovered
Human T-cell leukemia virus (HTLV-1)	1981
Human immunodeficiency virus (HIV, formally called HTLV-III)	1983
Xenotropic murine leukemia virus–related virus (XMRV) in prostate cancer cells	2006
Xenotropic murine leukemia virus–related virus (XMRV) in cells of CFS patients	2009

Taken from: CFIDS Association of America, "Known Retroviral Infections in Humans." www.cfids.org/webinar/xmrv-slides-jan2010.pdf.

ger by offering the $650 diagnostic test, 300 of which have been administered so far. Lombardi's group never claimed XMRV caused CFS, so it's not clear what a patient could do with a positive result. Lombardi argues that patients can avoid infecting other people with XMRV and have their diagnoses validated, if nothing else. His test results also bolster the science in the original paper—he says 36% of tests have detected XMRV, including a few from the United Kingdom.

To resolve the dispute, both sides say they are willing to work with the other and possibly test each other's samples. In the meantime, more papers exploring the link are slated to appear in the next few months, and each side says it knows of work supporting its hypothesis. Meanwhile, the field will continue to churn. As McClure told *Science*, "We take no pleasure in finding colleagues wrong or dashing the hopes of patients, but it's imperative the truth gets out."

A Virus-Caused CFS Could Have Troubling Public Health Implications

Amy Dockser Marcus

In the following viewpoint reporter Amy Dockser Marcus discusses the August 2010 publication of evidence for the presence of the virus family that includes the virus XMRV in the blood of people with chronic fatigue syndrome (CFS). This has led some CFS patients to seek treatment with the drugs used to fight HIV, the virus that causes AIDS, and there has been a call for a large-scale clinical trial of these drugs. While XMRV and HIV are different, they are both retroviruses, a relatively rare type of virus in humans. It is not yet known, says the author, whether XMRV causes CFS or is merely associated with the disorder. It has also been found in prostate cancer patients and in 6.8 percent of apparently healthy blood donors, so scientists are not sure what the effects of the virus are. They are worried because if it is in the blood of the general population, then millions of people could be infected. Marcus is a staff reporter for the *Wall Street Journal* and the winner of the 2005 Pulitzer Prize for Beat Reporting.

SOURCE: Amy Dockser Marcus, "New Hope in Fatigue Fight," *Wall Street Journal,* August 24, 2010. Republished with permission of Wall Street Journal, conveyed through Copyright Clearance Center, Inc.

Researchers said they had identified a family of retroviruses in patients with chronic fatigue syndrome [CFS], opening up a potentially promising new avenue of treatment for a debilitating disease that afflicts as many as four million Americans and 17 million people world-wide.

The finding will likely spur patients with the condition to seek treatment with drugs used to fight HIV, the virus that causes AIDS. Although HIV and the newly identified virus group are different, they are both retroviruses.

The report, published in the *Proceedings of the National Academy of Sciences,* was accompanied by a call for new clinical trials to test HIV drugs in patients with chronic fatigue syndrome.

Doctors don't know what causes chronic fatigue syndrome, characterized by debilitating fatigue and chronic pain with symptoms that can wax and wane over time. Some patients say friends, co-workers and even family members don't believe they are really sick.

Studies finding a viral connection with the disease would completely transform how the illness is treated and viewed. The findings also offer a potential path for treatment, possibly with drugs that are already FDA- [Food and Drug Administration-]approved for another condition.

Based on other recent research linking the syndrome to a retrovirus called XMRV, some doctors are already prescribing drugs approved for HIV for fatigue patients. The syndrome has no effective treatments yet.

The group of viruses identified in fatigue patients, called murine leukemia virus-related viruses, or MLV, are known to cause cancer and neurological problems in mice, but whether they cause disease in humans isn't known. XMRV is among several different members of the MLV family, researchers said.

In the new study, researchers said they found at least one of four different MLV-like viruses in 32 of 37, or

This colored electron micrograph shows the murine leukemia virus (MLV) in purple. In a recent study, researchers found that MLV-like viruses were found in a majority of CFS subjects. (Dr. Gopal Murti/Photo Researchers, Inc.)

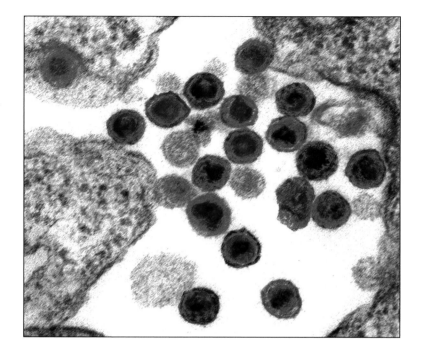

86.5%, of patients with chronic fatigue syndrome, compared with just three of 44, or 6.8%, of apparently healthy blood donors.

[The new study] is the latest in a series of reports about a possible link between CFS and a virus. Interest in viruses has been intense since an October report in the journal *Science* found XMRV in a majority of fatigue patients.

Subsequent studies have focused on XMRV and found conflicting evidence. Indeed, the just-published study was held back from publication in June because it was at odds with a report from the Centers for Disease Control and Prevention [CDC], which found no evidence of XMRV in chronic-fatigue-syndrome patients.

The current paper didn't find XMRV, either—one reason it isn't likely to resolve a brewing debate over the role XMRV may play in the syndrome.

But researchers said the variants of MLV-like viruses closely related to XMRV that they found in fatigue patients was evidence of a link between the virus family and the syndrome.

Anti-retroviral Drugs May Help

Andrew Mason, a University of Alberta professor, co-wrote the commentary in the journal calling for trials testing anti-retrovirals in CFS patients who are positive for one of the MLV-related viruses. "If the patients improve, after a certain point you stop debating whether it causes the disease and say, the treatment works and we're going to use it," said Dr. Mason.

But until scientists develop further evidence establishing that the virus causes the syndrome, a large-scale clinical trial testing HIV drugs against the ailment isn't likely. Norbert Bischofberger, chief scientific officer at Gilead Sciences Inc., the leading maker of HIV drugs, said the company might consider a small pilot trial but would like to see stronger evidence that the viruses cause CFS before launching a large trial. Still, "I'm very open, and this would be a great opportunity," he said.

A spokesman for Merck & Co., another major manufacturer of HIV drugs, said: "A clinical trial program would be possible to develop only after further substantial evidence of an association with CFS."

Some doctors and patients are already testing the idea, based in part on a University of Utah and Emory University study in cells. The compounds were tested singly and then in combinations of two at a time, and suggested that three anti-retroviral drugs appeared to inhibit infection by XMRV.

Jamie Deckoff-Jones, 56 years old, a doctor and CFS patient in New Mexico, has been blogging about her experiences and those of her 20-year-old daughter. Both tested positive for XMRV and are taking a combination of three anti-retrovirals.

> ## FAST FACT
>
> According to a November 2010 report in the *Wall Street Journal,* a new study is under way that aims to end the debate over whether XMRV is associated with CFS. At least three labs have agreed to test fresh blood samples.

Potential Role of XMRV in CFS

Infection of blood cells by XMRV (xenotropic murine leukemia virus-related virus) could contribute to immune system dysfunction, additional infection, and neurologic disease in chronic fatigue syndrome.

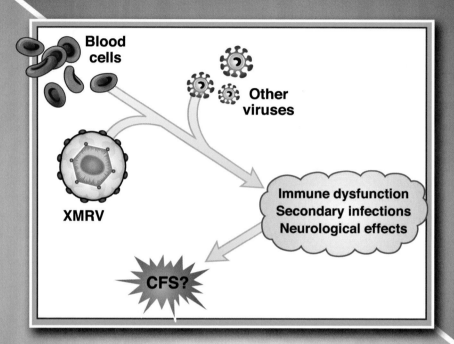

Taken from: Robert H. Silverman et al. "The Human Retrovirus XMRV in Prostate Cancer and Chronic Fatigue Syndrome," *Nature Reviews Urology* 7, July 2010. www.nature.com/nrurol/journal/v7/n7/fig_tab/nrurol.2010.77_F2.html.

Dr. Deckoff-Jones said a year ago she could only get up for short periods during the day. After five months on the drugs, she flew last week to Reno for an XMRV conference. Her daughter was able to go to a party and is enrolling in community college. "This is all very new, and there is no way to know if improvement will continue," Dr. Deckoff-Jones wrote in an email, "but we appear to be on an uphill course."

After the latest paper was held, the researchers took additional steps to demonstrate that the finding was related to a retrovirus and not lab contamination. Eight of the fatigue patients in the study who tested positive for an MLV-related virus using blood frozen 15 years ago were asked to come back to give fresh blood. Seven of the eight remained positive, and the virus had changed slightly over time, a characteristic of a retrovirus.

Many Questions Remain

Many questions remain on why different groups are coming up with different results. It is still unclear why the Centers for Disease Control didn't find XMRV or MLV-related viruses in its own study of fatigue patients. At a press briefing Monday, Steve Monroe, director of CDC's division of high-consequence pathogens and pathology, said that CDC was able to find MLV-related viruses in a small number of prostate cancer patients, data that isn't yet published.

Anthony L. Komaroff of Harvard Medical School, an author of the latest study, said one explanation may be that the patients used in the new study were chosen because they were very sick. Patients in other studies "are a very different group of people than the ones that knock on my door," he said.

Meantime, the finding that a small fraction of healthy blood donors may be harboring MLV-like virus raises new worries, researchers said. If confirmed and shown to reflect the presence of the virus in the broader population, it could mean that tens of millions of people in the U.S. and more world-wide are infected.

The implications aren't clear. Research has also linked XMRV to prostate cancer. People diagnosed with chronic fatigue syndrome are already barred from donating blood in Canada, Australia and New Zealand out of fear a virus may be passed on through transfusions.

AABB, a Bethesda, Md., organization whose members collect most blood donated in the U.S., advises that Americans with fatigue syndrome not donate blood until more data are available. A federally led working group is trying to determine how many blood donors may be infected.

[*Editor's note:* The American Red Cross has now banned donation of blood by CFS patients.]

Chronic Fatigue Syndrome Involves an Abnormal Genetic Response to Exercise

Deborah Rafferty

In the following viewpoint writer Deborah Rafferty discusses research published in 2009 by Alan Light, an anesthesiology professor at the University of Utah, that sheds new light on the reasons that patients with chronic fatigue syndrome (CFS) feel so fatigued after only a little exercise. He found that the genes responsible for telling muscles that they are too tired to keep working trigger this response much faster in CFS patients than it does in healthy people. This discovery, Rafferty says, will help to prove that CFS is a biological disorder and may, after more research, lead to a medical test for diagnosing it. Rafferty is a staff writer at the *Daily Utah Chronicle*.

A lan Light's new research into what causes fatigue has done anything but exhaust him.

Excited over the findings in his work, he animatedly described the intricacies of all the genes splashed across the cover of the *Journal of Pain* that published his

SOURCE: Deborah Rafferty, "U Researcher Helps Explain Chronic Fatigue," *Daily Utah Chronicle*, September 16, 2010. Reproduced by permission.

findings. The more a person exercises, the more a newly understood gene everyone has tells the body's muscles they are too tired to keep working—some to a debilitating degree, he said.

"It is surprising at the half-hour mark how much the gene increases in patients with chronic fatigue syndrome," said Light, an anesthesiology research professor, pointing to the differences between normal patients and patients with the disorder.

This research will allow patients with CFS to better understand what is happening to them and hopefully prove to the scientific world that it is an actual disease, not an excuse for what can be perceived as lazy behavior. It will also give physicians a test to determine if patients have CFS and how to provide proper treatment to help them get better.

The fatigue experienced by people afflicted with CFS makes it difficult for them to cope with everyday tasks. Even completing a set of simple exercises is taxing. (© **Glow Wellness/ Alamy**)

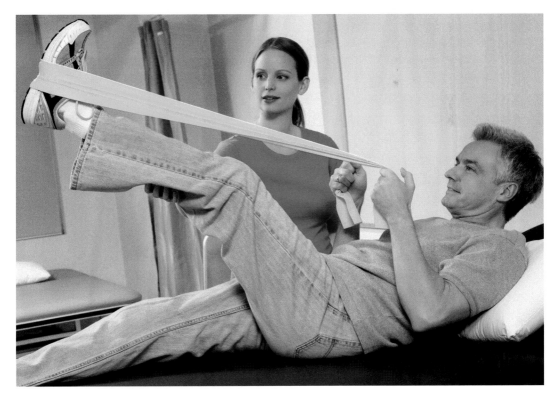

Light and his team of researchers identified a number of genes that increase during exercise in a ground-breaking discovery—especially for patients with CFS. These genes produce a protein, which tells the muscles they are tired and to stop exercising.

The experiments were first conducted using mouse models. However, the problem with the mice is that they cannot tell you whether they are in pain or are tired.

Blood Test After Exercise May Reveal CFS

In human trials, Light had two separate groups—people with and without CFS—do a simple arm and leg movement exercise for 25 minutes, which takes the same amount of energy as walking up stairs, Light said. Then they drew white blood cells from the patients at various points during the next 24 hours.

For the normal group, the patients had little trouble doing the exercise. However, the patients with CFS had extreme difficulty even finishing. Light said patients with CFS have trouble having enough energy to do everyday tasks and often do not leave the house. It's as though someone is screaming at you, and after a while, you stop listening, Light said. "Imagine that you have really beaten yourself [up] doing an exercise you haven't done in a while," Light said. "Imagine what you feel like the next day. Now imagine feeling like that all the time. That's what patients with CFS feel like."

After analyzing the data from the trials, Light and his researchers found that exercise increases the amount of the proteins that tell the muscles they are tired. Normal patients show very little change, but in patients with CFS there is a tremendous amount of proteins, which could explain why the patients are tired all the time, Light said. Most

> **FAST FACT**
>
> Studies at the University of South Wales in Australia in 2007 examined thirty thousand genes in blood samples from people who had had mononucleosis and found thirty-five genes that were expressed differently in those who recovered quickly from the illness, compared with those who developed CFS symptoms.

Increase in Certain Proteins After Exercise in People with and Without CFS

The colors indicate specific proteins produced by different genes that are involved in sensing muscle fatigue.

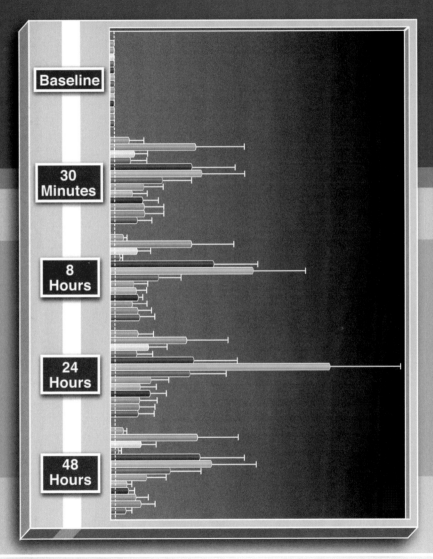

After twenty-five minutes of exercise, at the times indicated, all nineteen CFS patients reached 70 percent of the predicted maximal heart rate. After twenty-five minutes of exercise, the fifteen controls, at times, reached 70 percent of the predicted maximal heart rate.

Taken from: First CFIDS Webinar of 2010; Alan Light, unpublished data. www.cfids.org/webinar/xmrv-slides-jan2010.pdf.

of the genes Light identified were sensory, which tell the brain what the rest of the body is feeling.

For Light, the research has only just begun. He would like to analyze more [data about] what fatigue is and the difference between mental and physical fatigue. However, testing mental fatigue would be difficult because researchers could not extract brain cells because the cells do not grow back.

"What is fatigue? To most of the world, it is a sensation, something a little like pain," Light said. "It makes you want to stop what you are doing. Fatigue is a system in place to protect us from overusing our body and brain to prevent irreversible damage."

Patients with Myalgic Encephalomyelitis and CFS Are Treated Inequitably

Mary Schweitzer

In the following viewpoint Mary Schweitzer explains that, in 2008, during the transition to Barack Obama's presidency, various committees met to make recommendations about health-care policy. A group of myalgic encephalomyelitis/chronic fatigue syndrome (ME/CFS) patients submitted a report emphasizing that people with this disorder do not get fair treatment in comparison with patients with other illnesses. ME/CFS is not taken seriously by the government or the medical profession, the committee said, and there is prejudice against people who have it. Harm was done by adoption of the name *chronic fatigue syndrome,* which should be changed. A definition developed by practicing doctors should be adopted in place of the one intended only for research. Funding should be increased, the past misuse of government funds should be investigated, and it should be made easier for patients to get disability payments. There is an urgent need to act soon. Schweitzer is a former history professor who is seriously disabled by myalgic encephalomyelitis.

SOURCE: Mary Schweitzer, "*Obama–Biden Transition Project Health Care Community Discussion Report,*" cfids-me.org, December 30, 2008. Reproduced by permission.

W e are a small group of friends within a larger long-term online community of citizens who share one attribute: we are all disabled, significantly ill for a very long time, and we share the maddeningly inept diagnosis of "Chronic Fatigue Syndrome" (CFS)....

Our primary issue is the fundamental inequality in the treatment of patients who have the disease M.E. (Myalgic Encephalomyelitis) and/or have a diagnosis of Chronic Fatigue Syndrome....

We were asked to examine health care in the United States and how best to reform it. Unfortunately, it matters little whether you have the best health insurance available or none at all, if you have been rendered an invalid by a condition kept invisible by the actions of NIH [National Institutes of Health] and CDC [Centers for Disease Control and Prevention].

Medical doctors and other medical personnel are members of a larger society and culture in the United States. No matter the extent of professional training, popular beliefs and perceptions will subconsciously influence their behavior. In the absence of information about the depth and severity of our illness, popular norms dominate the attitude that greets us when we walk into a doctor's office or an emergency room.

In a nation where everyone is overworked and hence "a little tired," where the word "chronic" is associated with such terms as "chronic whiner" and "chronic complainer," and the word "syndrome" has become code for "fad of the day," NIH and CDC could not have picked a better way to describe a disease that—quite bluntly—they apparently wish would disappear on its own.

This might have been understandable 25 years ago when a number of cluster outbreaks of the disease occurred in the midst of the AIDS crisis that overwhelmed the medical establishment. Today, however, there are thousands of peer-reviewed research articles into the biological causation of many of the symptoms, and subgroups have been defined through objective testing: biomarkers, SPECT [brain] scans, and specific types of stress tests. . . .

Yet the NIH and CDC have continued to focus on "psychosocial" research, not biomedical. . . .

Many CFS patients test positive for reactivated viruses. . . . Some have tested positive for mycoplasma [fungal infection]; and some test positive for Lyme as well. For these patients, immune, antiviral, and on occasion antibiotic treatment is necessary. But if doctors do not know about these tests, no one will receive the treatments.

CFS Is Not Taken Seriously

It should be no surprise that, 25 years after the first effort by CDC to study the phenomenon of "CFS," 85 percent of patients today still have no diagnosis (according to CDC). Of those who have a diagnosis, even fewer have a doctor who understands it. And because this disease is so poorly understood, many who do have a diagnosis of CFS have no symptoms resembling ours.

It if is popularly believed that a condition is pretty normal, experienced by everyone at some point in time (fatigue), then having an illness defined by that condition is hardly reason for alarm—hardly reason for urgency—and hardly an excuse for not working. More to the point, it is no reason to spend money—a position that makes the insurance lobbyists on K-Street [in Washington, DC,] happy, and also pleases those within the government who believe that catering to "entitlements" are a main reason for "high" government spending. Keeping one million patients hidden from view (because of the extent of our disability) has served political purposes that hopefully will change in the Obama presidency.

The name "chronic fatigue syndrome," however well-intentioned, subliminally accomplishes this mission. No one takes this disease seriously—no one, except those of us who have been saddled with the diagnosis, and our families.

The CDC has become adept at presenting one position on CFS to patient groups, another to physicians, and yet another to Congress. On the one hand, their own literature states that "CFS is a debilitating and complex disorder." Conversely, they have dismissed outright every biomarker that has been discovered with regard to the cluster outbreak patients of the mid-1980s. Their own "CFS Toolkit for Professionals," devotes an entire section to "cognitive behavior therapy" (psychotherapy) and another section to "graded exercise." The introduction to the CDC Toolkit states, "As yet, there are no diagnostic tests or laboratory markers for CFS, and its pathophysiology is unknown." . . .

The Situation for Patients with ME/CFS

1. People with very serious conditions are misdiagnosed, and a misdiagnosis leads to improper treatment, or no treatment at all. Simple example: a patient with Hepatitis C will be misdiagnosed as having CFS and not receive treatment for hepatitis. Conversely, if a patient has CFS because he/she has an immune defect and viruses, "cognitive behavior therapy" (as recommended by CDC) is not going to be much help, and if a patient has encephalitis or myocarditis, graded exercise (as recommended by CDC) can be dangerous.

2. Even well-intentioned and caring family doctors are baffled by patients with a CFS diagnosis who "refuse to get well"—who do not get better, or even get worse. It makes doctors uncomfortable. A patient with a CFS diagnosis can be reasonably expected to have other things go wrong with their bodies—acute appendicitis, for example—but their family doctor may be "burned out" on having to listen to symptoms that he/she cannot fix. The case of acute appendicitis gets dismissed as "yet another one of those symptoms" for this fuzzy thing called CFS—and the prob-

lem may not be resolved until the patient is in the hospital with peritonitis. . . .

3. Nobody really believes that somebody with "CFS" can't work. Everyone's tired. Why should one person who claims to be tired get off work when other people who are tired have to remain? Of course, those of us diagnosed with "CFS" are not just "tired"—we have the level of fatigue that is normally associated with congestive heart failure or leukemia. As Dan Peterson noted in the documentary "I Remember Me," his CFS patients are as seriously ill as AIDS patients in the last two months of life. The popular perception that we are "just tired" obviously makes it incredibly difficult to receive either public or private disability. . . . We know that at least one million Americans currently have this disease. Based upon research by the CDC, which historically has downplayed the severity of this disease, we know that at least half of them cannot work at all at any given point in time. That would mean that *500,000 Americans (most of whom have no diagnosis) are completely and utterly incapable of paid work because they have "CFS."* Few receive SSDI [Social Security Disability Insurance]; even fewer receive private long-term disability. The rest must depend upon family members, and if they have none, their situation is desperate. We all have known of patients who have had to live on the street. How many more are there?

4. If you are denied disability, you are also denied medical care. Admittedly, private insurance and Medicare will not pay for testing and treatment for "CFS." However, there are a number of comorbidities [accompanying diseases] that are recognized by CDC, and (as in the appendicitis example), CFS patients can be expected to have the same general physical problems (such

> **FAST FACT**
>
> On October 14, 2010, the Chronic Fatigue Syndrome Advisory Committee of the US Department of Health and Human Services unanimously endorsed a recommendation that the government change the name of chronic fatigue syndrome (CFS) to ME/CFS because of the need to make clear that the disorder is more serious than mere fatigue.

Individuals with CFS are not merely overtired; they have a level of exhaustion comparable to that experienced by patients with congestive heart failure or leukemia. (© Catchlight Visual Services/Alamy)

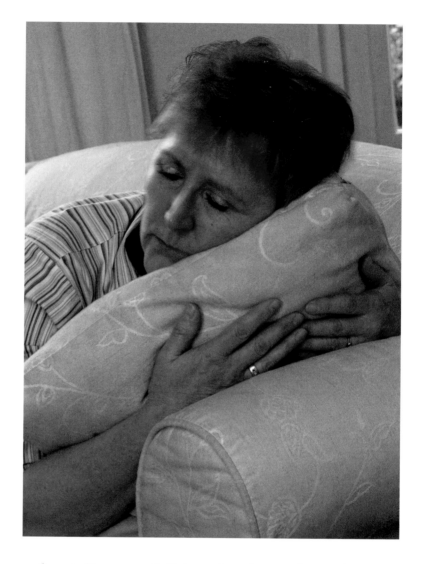

as heart disease and diabetes) and experience the same acute problems (such as a diseased gallbladder or appendix) as the normal population—but if you do not have insurance, it is very difficult to get help.

5. Prejudice against patients "claiming CFS" can infect everyone from family members to neighbors to church groups. During the years that I ran a supportive on-line discussion list (averaging about 500 members at any given point in time), I knew patients who had been

cast out by spouses or parents, scolded and disdained by siblings, and even abandoned by their churches.

6. Here we are, a quarter of a century after the set of cluster outbreaks in the 1980s that led to the name "chronic fatigue syndrome" adopted by CDC and NIH, and there simply are no doctors who can treat a patient with the disease. . . .

I don't know what to tell patients. The only doctors I know who have specialized in this disease have retired, left their practice to focus on research, or closed their practices to newcomers because they are so overwhelmed.

7. Changing the name from Myalgic Encephalomyelitis (as it was known in Canada, Australia, and Britain) and Epidemic Neuromyasthenia (as it was known in the United States—or for that matter, "chronic Epstein-Barr Virus," the name NIH first gave to the disease, to "chronic fatigue syndrome," has had international consequences. British psychiatrists picked it up and have successfully convinced British public health that CFS and M.E. are the same thing. But they do not use the same definition for CFS as the U.S. Their definition is entirely psychological, and all they offer for treatment is ten weeks of "cognitive behaviour therapy (CBT)" to convince the patient she isn't really sick, followed by ten weeks of "graded exercise therapy (GET)" to get her back up to speed. They believe the disease should really be called "neurasthenia"—the nervous disease diagnosed back in the 1800s. M.E. was classified as a neurological illness by WHO [World Health Organization] in the late 1960s, so British psychiatrists have thus far failed in their efforts to reclassify the disease as a neurosis.

Nevertheless, the consequences of applying the name CFS to a psychiatric diagnosis have been horrendous. Patients who once could get treatment can no longer find a caregiver. Schoolchildren, young adults, and even a vocal critic of the NICE [National Institute for Health and Clinical Excellence] guidelines have been "sectioned"—involuntarily committed to psychiatric hospitals. The result has been greater disability (patients who could walk are reduced to needing a wheelchair) and death, including two recent deaths of young people. . . .

The Government Should Take Positive Action

1. There needs to be a sense of urgency. For 25 years patients have suffered from this illness. It is contagious at some point in its course. Consequently, every year there are more sufferers as the disease (or diseases) spreads unabated. At what point do we ask the CDC to stop conducting population studies and begin to educate the public as to biomarkers, objective testing (not questionnaires), and treatment? . . .

2. Change the name. The CDC claims to be waiting for a name chosen by "medical science." Yet the name "CFS" represents an arbitrary name change from the known diagnosis of epidemic neuromyasthenia in the U.S., and Myalgic Encephalomyelitis in the old British Empire. . . . There is no reason to keep this artificial name, which has dramatically failed to accomplish much that is positive. Better alternatives for a name would be:

   (a) to adopt the name that has been in continuous use for 50 years internationally, Myalgic Encephalomyelitis;

   (b) compromise: adopt the designation in the World Health Organization's current International Classification of Diseases—"ICD-10", in which "CFS" is classified in G93.3, the code created for Myalgic Encephalomyelitis in the late 1960s. Call the disease ME/CFS, until people get used to the name M.E. or until a new name emerges from research.

   (c) acknowledge the complexity of the illness by giving a name that includes the multiple systems impacted by the disease: neurologic, immune, endocrine, cardio. One example is: neuroendocrineimmune disorders. One advantage is that the name leaves room to carve out subgroups that would get their own name. . . . Another would be that there are probably other disorders that already could be included under this name, such as fibromyalgia, multiple chemical sensitivities, Lyme Disease, and Gulf War Syndrome.

(d) create an eponym [the name of a person who has the disease] as was done with Lou Gehrig's disease (ALS [amyotrophic lateral sclerosis]). . . .

3. Change the definition. . . .

Adopt the definition from the Canadian Consensus Document for ME/CFS until we learn more about the disease (or diseases). The committee that created this document consisted of clinical practitioners, and about half practice in the United States. All the other definitions created for "chronic fatigue syndrome" were explicitly designed for research. This is the only definition designed for clinical use, and it offers a means of recognizing the complexity of the condition at the same time it presents options to begin treating it. . . .

4. Change the diagnostic procedure. Make it clear that this is not an easy condition to diagnose, and that the usual 5–10 minute limitation given doctors by insurance companies is simply not adequate. . . .

5. Inform doctors about the diagnostic testing available now, and require that at least Medicare pay for them. There are immune markers that are found in subgroups of CFS patients and nobody else. There are viruses that we did not know about 25 years ago, but we know about now. . . .

6. Fund Centers of Excellence where family doctors can send patients suspected of having ME/CFS. Given the complexity of the illness, and the wealth of information that is emerging internationally, it is impractical to ask family doctors to keep abreast of this disease—as they cannot keep abreast of other complex diseases such as cancers. . . .

7. Fund external and internal research into biomarkers and treatments ASAP [as soon as possible]. The Whittemore-Peterson Institute for Neuroimmune Diseases in Reno, Nevada, has only been open two years [as of 2008], but it has already produced more hard research than either CDC or NIH in 25 years. The NIH has allocated little if any funding for the disease in the past few years. . . .

8. We strongly urge a formal investigation by the GAO [US Government Accountability Office] into the use of funding by both NIH and CDC with regard to CFS. Several members of this committee have hard evidence into abuse of funding by these two agencies. Patient groups have testified to these abuses at the CFSAC [Chronic Fatigue Syndrome Advisory Committee] meetings, to no avail. . . .

9. Revise the information given by the SSA [Social Security Administration] to intake workers and physicians, and reduce the time it takes to receive disability. As objective markers become approved, advise the SSA immediately. In the meantime, the entire Social Security system should act according to court rulings that state clearly that no one should be denied coverage on the basis of the absence of testing, while the CDC insists there are no tests. . . .

10. Decide whether disability and health insurance companies are going to be regulated locally or federally. If federally . . . then *regulate them.* Surely the events of the past year have shown that industries that deal in information need to be regulated. There is a perverse incentive for disability and health insurance companies to cheat the patient as long as no one checks up on their activities. The insurance companies even have a name for dismissing diseases such as "chronic fatigue syndrome"—they call them "MUS" disorders—"medically unexplained symptoms," which (even if true, which it is not), should not be synonymous with "imaginary." . . .

Comparative Government Research Funding

Chronic fatigue syndrome affects more people than many other diseases to which the government devotes more research money.

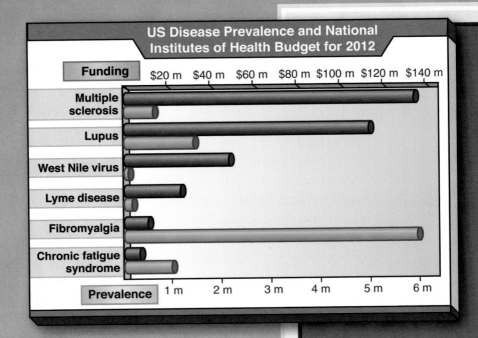

US Disease Prevalence and National Institutes of Health Budget for 2012

Multiple sclerosis: Funding, $135 million; 500,000 Americans with this condition

Lupus: $114 million; 1.5 million Americans

West Nile virus: $46 million; 3,630 Americans (2007)

Lyme disease: $25 million; 150,000 Americans (since 1992)

Fibromyalgia: $9 million; 3–6 million Americans

Chronic fatigue syndrome: $6 million; 1 million Americans

Taken from: ME/CFS Worldwide Patient Alliance, "Government Resources Funding: NIH Budget for 2012 and Disease Prevalence," http://mcwpa.org/resrouces/research-funding-comparison. Source: NiH Funding, http://report.nih.gov/rcdc/categories.

"The Fierce Urgency of Now"

President Obama spoke of "the fierce urgency of now." I cannot imagine anything more urgent than to rescue people who are suffering, and dying, from a disease rendered invisible by the federal government of the United States. The need for care is urgent. The need for research is urgent. Our disease has been allowed to fester untreated in the community for 25 years, causing immeasurable loss to individuals, families, and society at large. On some level this disease is contagious. If nothing else, we need to stop its spread.

Preparing this report has taken us weeks, because we are all quite disabled. . . . Three members had to drop out of the effort before it was over. But we are speaking for a million Americans—perhaps more importantly, we are speaking for at least 850,000 Americans who have our disease but have no diagnosis. We could not be silent, no matter the personal cost.

As late as the 1960s, patients suffering from Multiple Sclerosis were misdiagnosed as having "hysterical paralysis." A woman with MS would be told to "shape up"—go back to her role as housewife and mother and take care of the kids. If she could not, it was somehow *her* fault.

A similar pattern of cruelty is being inflicted on patients with ME/CFS in the United States, simply because the NIH/CDC–approved research has not caught up with the severity of the disease. It is absurd that patients should be penalized because of an assumption that there is nothing left to learn about the human body—but even that sad period in our nation's medical history can be brought to a close. We already know enough about ME/CFS to stop the inhumanity and begin to appropriately deal with patients and their suffering. All that is lacking is the will.

The need to face this disease squarely and honestly is *urgent*, and it is urgent *now*.

Common Medical or Psychiatric Conditions Are Usually the Cause of Chronic Fatigue

Samuel B. Harvey and Simon Wessely

In the following viewpoint Samuel B. Harvey and Simon Wessley say that because there are no biological tests that can confirm or rule out a diagnosis of chronic fatigue syndrome (CFS), doctors spend a long time looking for other explanations of a person's illness before deciding that he or she has CFS. But studies have shown that most cases of fatigue can be attributed to common medical or psychiatric conditions, which the authors believe means that delays caused by looking for more unusual conditions are unjustified. CFS is usually brought on by psychological factors—even if a medical condition triggers it—and so the underlying cause makes little difference to treatment. They argue that psychological treatment is the most effective way of dealing with CFS and that treatment should begin as soon as possible. Harvey is a clinical lecturer in the Department of Psychological Medicine at the Institute of Psychiatry, King's College London. Wessely, the head of that department, is an influential British psychiatrist known for his belief that CFS is a psychological disorder.

SOURCE: Samuel B. Harvey and Simon Wessely, "Chronic Fatigue Syndrome: Identifying Zebras Amongst the Horses," *BMC Medicine,* October 12, 2009. Copyright © 2009 Harvey and Wessely; licensee BioMed Central Ltd. Reproduced by permission.

Medical students are often told that the sound of approaching hooves is more likely to herald the arrival of horses than zebras. The metaphor reinforces the idea that in medicine common things happen commonly and that clinicians should avoid spending too much time chasing rare or unlikely diagnoses. Fatigue is a very common clinical problem with many possible causes. Some causes of fatigue are common 'horses' such as anaemia, viral infections, sleep deprivation, diabetes and depression. However, potential 'zebras' such as malignancy or auto-immune disorders may also present with fatigue. Even with extensive investigations, the underlying aetiology [cause] of an individual's fatigue in many cases remains unknown. Over recent decades there has been increasing recognition of a group of individuals with severe, persistent, and unexplained fatigue. Such persistent fatigue has, at times, been seen as an illness of modern life, although there is good evidence to show that chronic fatigue has been a common problem since at least the 19th century, but under different diagnostic labels, such as neurasthenia. Some, but by no means all, of these individuals fulfil the current criteria for chronic fatigue syndrome (CFS), which requires that persisting or relapsing fatigue be present for at least 6 months, is not relieved by rest, is not explained by medical or psychiatric conditions and is accompanied by a range of cognitive and somatic [physical] symptoms. Here, we discuss a paper by [J.] Jones *et al.* published this month [October 2009] in *BMC Medicine*, as well as recent prospective studies that provide valuable insights into the aetiology and contribute to a model for understanding chronic fatigue.

At present, and despite much effort, there are no investigative tools or physical signs that can confirm the presence of CFS and it remains a diagnosis of exclusion. As a result, clinicians must decide how long to keep looking

FAST FACT

According to the Worldwide Association for ME/CFS Awareness and Research, an estimated 28 million people worldwide suffer from ME/CFS.

for alternative explanations for fatigue before settling on a diagnosis of CFS. There are numerous cautionary tales of individuals who have suffered from delayed or missed diagnoses of serious illnesses due to underinvestigating of fatigue. Yet if the search for unlikely 'zebra' causes of fatigue goes on too long, the risk of iatrogenic harm [harm caused by a doctor's actions] increases and the opportunity for early focused treatment of CFS may be lost.

Chronic Fatigue Is Often Caused by Common Conditions

Studies based in specialized clinics have suggested that yields from detailed investigations of those with prolonged fatigue are low, with only 5% of laboratory tests revealing an underlying cause. However, fatigued patients seen in specialized clinics differ from those seen in other settings, with some reports suggesting higher yields from investigations may be possible in primary care. The recently published VAMPIRE study based in Dutch primary care found that 8% of patients presenting with fatigue had a blood test—detectable somatic illness diagnosed over a 1-year follow-up period, with the vast majority of the disorders identified from a very limited set of simple blood tests. . . . The UK–based National Institute of Health and Clinical Excellence guidelines on the diagnosis and management of CFS recommend a slightly more conservative approach, with a more extensive list of blood and urine investigations suggested. Such lists of physical investigations should not detract from the need to consider psychological causes of fatigue. Depression is very common amongst those with fatigue, with recent studies using the British birth cohorts showing over 70% of adults reporting CFS have evidence of psychiatric disorder prior to their fatigue symptoms beginning.

A clinician assessing a patient in the community with apparent CFS may well ask 'If I look, how likely am I to find a contributing medical or psychiatric cause for the

Studies in the United Kingdom have found depression to be common among those with fatigue. In one such study, 70 percent of adults reporting CFS were found to have had a psychiatric disorder prior to the onset of their fatigue symptoms. (**LADA/ Photo Researchers, Inc.**)

fatigue, and what difference will this make?' A paper by Jones *et al.* may help to answer these questions. Using random telephone surveys, 904 people who met the criteria for CFS were identified. On telephone history alone they were able to identify a potential cause of the fatigue in 441 (48%). When the remaining cases were seen for a physical examination, psychiatric interview and laboratory screening, potential medical or psychiatric causes of fatigue were identified in a further 49%. Not surprisingly, the most common co-morbid conditions identified were depression, followed by bipolar affective disorder, thyroid disease, substance misuse and diabetes. Obesity, already known to be associated with a number of these conditions, increased the chances of a medical or psychiatric cause being identified. These results are very similar to a Dutch study published earlier this year, which found concomitant diseases which could cause fatigue in 55.5% of those reporting chronic fatigue lasting more than 6 months. Based on these findings, clinicians should feel encouraged that, if they look for common psychiatric and medical conditions in those complaining of prolonged fatigue, the rate of detection will be higher than previously thought. Thus, current recommendations advising a range of simple investigations for those with persistent fatigue seem well placed. Jones *et al.* did find some 'zebras' but, as expected, these were relatively rare. A simple mental state examination appears to remain the most productive single investigation in any new person presenting with unexplained fatigue.

Cause of CFS Makes Little Difference to Treatment

The identification of potentially treatable causes of fatigue has obvious clinical importance. However, Jones *et al.*'s findings also raise questions about the nature of chronic fatigue. Currently, most diagnostic criteria suggest CFS should not be diagnosed when an active medical or psychiatric condition is identified which may explain the fatigue. This implies that the aetiology of 'unexplained' CFS is different to that of the 'explained' fatigue seen in those with a diagnosed medical condition. While we are yet to fully understand the causes of CFS, a number of prospective studies have given us some knowledge of those at high risk, and which pathways to fatigue seem to be important. Based on these findings, a model of the aetiology of CFS can be constructed. This suggests that CFS results from a combination of pre-morbid risk, followed by an acute event leading to fatigue, and then a pattern of behavioural and biological responses contributing to a prolonged severe fatigue syndrome. Based on this model, the initial cause of the fatigue has a limited impact on the eventual course of the illness. Rather, it is the maintaining factors, such as dramatic fluctuations in levels of activity (so called 'boom and bust' cycles), that need to be addressed if recovery is to occur. This model has been developed from research focused on the 'unex-

Related Conditions Associated with CFS

Chronic fatigue syndrome
Unrefreshing sleep
Headaches

Anxiety
Panic attacks
Avoidant behavior

Depression
Loss of motivation
Loss of pleasure

Prolonged fatigue states
Fatigue
Pain
Poor concentration
Irritable mood

Fibromyalgia
Muscle and joint pain
Tender points

Irritable bowel syndrome
Diarrhea/constipation
Abdominal pain
Bloating

Taken from: Liz Highleyman, "Chronic Fatigue Syndrome Linked to Infectious Retrovirus XMRV," October 13, 2009. www.hivandhepatitis.com.

plained' fatigue of CFS. However, there is emerging evidence which suggests that it may be appropriate to extend it to encompass fatigue with an apparent medical cause. There are numerous examples of studies demonstrating that the fatigue associated with clear 'physical' illnesses is more closely associated with behavioural and psychological factors than with the severity of the underlying illness. For example, fatigue in HIV-infected patients is more strongly associated with psychological factors than with measures of HIV disease progression or the use of highly active antiretroviral drugs. There is also evidence that behaviourally focused interventions are some of the most effective ways of reducing fatigue, even when there is a clear underlying cause, such as rheumatoid arthritis, multiple sclerosis or cancer. Thus, it may be that the divide between fatigue secondary to diagnosed medical problems and CFS may need to be made more permeable, with some relaxing of the exclusion criteria in diagnostic guidelines for CFS. This may allow a greater use of evidence-based treatments developed for treating CFS amongst those with an apparent medical or psychiatric cause of their fatigue.

Psychological Factors Can Produce Physical Disorders

Christine Heim

Despite thousands of research studies, the cause of chronic fatigue syndrome (CFS) remains unknown and is surrounded by controversy. In the following viewpoint Christine Heim says that there is evidence that both biological and psychological factors may contribute to CFS, yet people continue to argue that it is entirely one or the other. Both physical and emotional stress are known to physically affect the central nervous system, the neuroendocrine system, and the immune systems, and research in neuroscience centering on this fact may help to overcome the reluctance to believe that both are involved. For example, the author proposes that because childhood trauma can have permanent physical effects on the central nervous system while it is developing, it may produce vulnerability to CFS by altering the brain. Eventually, she says, CFS may be found to have an identifiable biological cause at the brain level, thus showing that psychological and physical interpretations of the illness are not mutually exclusive. Heim is an associate professor in the Department of Psychiatry and Behavioral Sciences at Emory University School of Medicine in Atlanta, Georgia.

SOURCE: Christine Heim, "New Perspective on Chronic Fatigue Syndrome: Lessons from Developmental Neuroscience," *Future Neurology*, vol. 4, 2009. Copyright © 2009 Future Medicine Ltd. Reproduced by permission.

Hardly ever has a somatic [physical] disorder been surrounded with as much controversy as chronic fatigue syndrome (CFS). Some people believe that the disorder does not even exist and consider CFS a classic manifestation of [Sigmund] Freud's concept of hysteria, which implies the unconscious simulation of organic disorders, in the context of emotional excitability, high anxiety, and sensory and motor disturbances. Of note, Freud thought that hysteria is brought about by an infantile traumatic experience. At the other end of the spectrum, patient representative groups often vividly advocate CFS as a true medical disease with a sole physiologic cause that, once pinned down, may hopefully be reversible using standard medical techniques in the future.

Facts About Chronic Fatigue Syndrome

In an effort to promote CFS as a legitimate medical condition, a nationwide public awareness campaign has recently been launched in the USA, with the aim to dissolve existing myths that surround CFS and educate the public regarding CFS facts. What are some of these facts? First and foremost, the condition is very common with up to 2.5% of the population suffering from CFS in the USA. CFS affects four-times more women than men, and most cases are middle-aged individuals. The average duration of CFS in cases identified from the population is 5–7 years, but less than 20% have been diagnosed with CFS by a physician. A quarter of affected individuals are unemployed or receive disability benefit and the average household forgoes US $20,000 in lost earnings and wages as a result of CFS. The total economic cost of CFS in the USA is an estimated $9.1 billion per year. Without doubt, CFS is a debilitating condition that is associated with considerable personal suffering and decreased quality of life for affected individuals.

Despite the magnitude of the public health problem, the causes of CFS remain unknown and specific targets for prevention and treatment remain elusive. To date, more than 4000 research studies have failed to identify a unanimous cause of CFS and there is evidence that both biological and psychological factors contribute to CFS. Reported biological abnormalities in CFS mostly affect the brain's regulatory outflow systems, namely, the endocrine, autonomic and immune systems. Psychological or behavioral factors contributing to the development or maintenance of CFS include inactivity, avoidance behavior, anxiety sensitivity and stress. High rates of psychiatric comorbidity have been reported for cases with CFS. Behavioral interventions, such as cognitive-behavioral therapy and graded exercise, are among the most effective treatments for CFS, perhaps providing the strongest support for the importance of psychological factors in CFS.

Patients and clinicians often point out that physical, emotional or chemical stressors trigger the onset of CFS symptoms, an impression also supported by research. As early as in the 1930s, Hans Selye, who first coined the term 'stress', proposed that psychological stress elicits a physiologic response, which he recognized to be adaptive, but that failure of physiological adaptation to stress, or exhaustion of the system, could result in disease. Nowadays, we know that stress exerts multiple effects on the central nervous, neuroendocrine, autonomic and immune systems that help an organism adapt to challenge. However, much less is known regarding why some individuals fail to adapt, resulting in functional changes that lead to symptoms, such as fatigue, pain, cognitive impairment and sleep disruption, combined with emotional problems. In order to understand CFS, it is of critical importance to understand sources of individual differences in the vulnerability to the pathogenic effects of stress.

Childhood Trauma May Be a Risk Factor for CFS

This article discusses results from two recent studies emphasizing the role of childhood trauma in CFS. Childhood trauma might be a vulnerability factor that interferes with successful adaptation to stress, thereby conveying a risk to developing CFS. Indeed, there is substantial plasticity of the developing CNS as a function of experience. During such critical periods, certain brain regions are also particularly sensitive to adverse experiences, which may then lead to major, sometimes irreversible, changes. Animal studies, pioneered by the late Seymour Levine, provide direct evidence that early adversity permanently programs neural circuits that are involved in regulating the adaptation of physiologic systems and behavioral responses to the environment, by inducing functional, structural and even epigenetic changes [changes in gene activation] in these circuits. Among the consequences of early-life stress in animal models and human studies, are many changes that resemble key features of CFS, including decreased basal cortisol secretion, increased immune activation, pain sensitivity, impaired cognition and altered sleep. Most recently, it has been ascertained in human post-mortem brain tissue obtained from suicide victims that early adversity . . . modifies endocrine stress reactivity and behavior.

Applying the general principle to CFS, it may be proposed that CFS indeed has an identifiable biological basis, which, albeit unknown, is most likely located at the brain level. At least in some affected individuals, this neurobiological basis may have been shaped by early experience, perhaps in interaction with other factors. As a consequence, the vulnerable brain may inadequately process and/or fail to adapt to emotional, physical or even chemical challenges, thereby producing the often

> **FAST FACT**
>
> According to a British study published in 2007, the claim that ME/CFS is the same as the "burnout" found in athletes is not valid because the changes in cortisol levels in burnout cases are the opposite of those found in patients with ME.

described physiological and behavioral characteristics that form the clinical phenotype of CFS. Clearly, considered from a developmental neuroscience perspective, supported by basic research, it becomes evident that the seemingly disparate points of view regarding the nature of CFS, that is to say psychological versus biological, are not mutually exclusive and that the diverse findings produced by CFS research may well be integrated in a developmental pathway model. Indeed, this perspective offers a new opportunity to reconcile some of the controversy surrounding CFS.

In order to start testing this assumption, it must be demonstrated that; first, early adverse experience is a risk factor for CFS and; second, that this risk factor is associated with a cardinal biological feature of CFS. Towards that end, the CDC [Centers for Disease Control and Prevention] (Atlanta, GA, USA) in collaboration with Emory University (Atlanta, GA, USA) recently conducted two population-based studies of CFS cases and controls. The first study employed a sample of 43 clinically confirmed cases with current CFS and 60 controls identified from a general population sample of 56,146 adult residents in Wichita, KS, USA. CFS cases reported significantly higher levels of childhood sexual, physical and emotional abuse, as well as emotional and physical neglect compared with controls. Exposure to childhood trauma was associated with a three- to eight-fold increased risk for CFS, depending on trauma type. Emotional neglect and sexual abuse were the best predictors of CFS. There was a graded relationship between degree of exposure and CFS risk. Childhood trauma was further associated with CFS symptom severity, and with depression, anxiety and post-traumatic stress disorder (PTSD) symptoms. While childhood trauma was ascertained as an independent risk factor for CFS, even in the absence of significant psychopathology, the risk of CFS conveyed by childhood trauma increased with the presence of concurrent psychopathology. These results provided support for childhood trauma as an important risk factor of CFS, partly mediated through an altered emotional state. . . .

CFS May Be Caused by Cortisol Deficiency

In a second study, our group closely replicated the above findings in an independent sample of CFS cases and controls identified from the general population in Georgia, USA. Results of this second study confirmed that emotional maltreatment, and sexual abuse in particular, are potent risk factors of CFS. The risk of having CFS increased to ninefold in the presence of concurrent PTSD

Research has shown that childhood trauma may create a vulnerability factor that interferes with successful adaptation to stress and that may contribute to a possible risk of developing CFS (© Cultura RM/Alamy)

symptoms. We then tested whether childhood trauma is associated with a cardinal biological feature of CFS in this sample. One of the hallmark features of CFS is . . . lower-than-normal cortisol secretion. Relative hypocortisolism has been observed as a correlate of early-life stress in non-human primates and humans, and is also a prominent feature of PTSD. In our study, the CFS group, as a whole, had flattened cortisol levels in response to awakening, in accordance with the general CFS literature. Only when stratifying groups by childhood trauma, it emerged that decreased cortisol secretion in CFS, in fact, was associated with childhood trauma, whereas CFS cases with no childhood trauma, exhibited normal cortisol levels. These results suggested that relative hypocortisolism in CFS, frequently described in the literature, may reflect a biological marker of risk of developing CFS, secondary to childhood trauma, rather than reflecting a correlate of the disorder itself. Similar associations appear to exist with other biological changes in CFS—for example, altered autonomic [nervous system] function.

Although unequivocal evidence for the importance of developmental factors in CFS must come from longitudinal studies [studies extended over a period of time], the current data provide important cues regarding potential disease mechanisms and the nature of comorbidity [accompanying disease], resilience factors, illness subtypes and intervention strategies related to CFS. Regarding mechanisms, a reduced effect of cortisol as a potential consequence of childhood trauma may be directly and causally linked to several of the key features of CFS; . . . reduced cortisol effects may decrease the organism's energy resources during stress, leading to exhaustion and fatigue. Cortisol further exerts regulatory effects on the immune system and helps reduce inflammatory responses to challenge. A lack of these cortisol functions may induce an inflammation-like state, promoting fatigue, pain and cognitive prob-

CFS Overlaps with Other Conditions

Some people have CFS along with other disorders, but not everyone with both prolonged fatigue and another disorder has CFS.

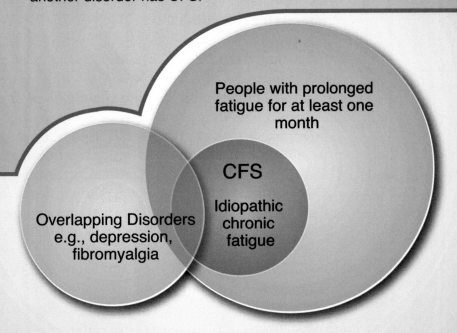

People with prolonged fatigue for at least one month

CFS

Idiopathic chronic fatigue

Overlapping Disorders e.g., depression, fibromyalgia

Taken from: Centers for Disease Control and Prevention, "Patient Examination Process for CFS, Step 7," Chronic Fatigue Syndrome. www.cdc.gov/cfs/general/diagnosis/diagnosis_process7.html.

lems. Lastly, cortisol has inhibitory effects on stress and emotion systems in the brain. Reduced cortisol effects may thus promote sensitization to stress and anxiety. The combined effects of relative cortisol deficiency might thus promote the symptom complex of CFS and might also explain comorbidity with emotional disorders, based on overlapping pathways.

Consequently, in terms of resilience factors, maintaining normal cortisol function after childhood trauma may protect against CFS and other disorders. . . . Interventions that . . . restore cortisol function may be effective in the prevention or treatment of CFS in children or adults who have experienced early trauma.

Different Types of CFS Have Different Causes

A final implication of the above results is that CFS is clearly a heterogeneous disorder. There appears to be subgroups of CFS as a function of childhood trauma that are biologically distinguishable. Approximately 60% of our sample reported at least one form of childhood adversity, while 40% did not. Changes in neuroendocrine function were limited to the subgroup of CFS cases with childhood trauma histories. The other 40% had normal cortisol levels, but still suffered from CFS. Perhaps, in analogy to historic approaches to depression classification, the latter group suffers from a more 'endogenous' form of CFS that did not develop in reaction to an environmental event and, therefore, is not associated with altered stress hormone secretion. In fact, there might be even further subgroups not captured by our study design. Thus, an important area for future research is to better define subgroups of CFS and scrutinize diverse mechanisms that may lead to the same clinical picture.

The recognition that there are different subgroups of CFS with different pathophysiologic pathways also helps explain inconsistent findings regarding mechanisms and treatment efficacy in the field. For example, disregarding childhood trauma histories alone likely has significantly confounded previous research on neuroendocrine function in CFS, as demonstrated above. Defining CFS subgroups might also allow for selecting optimal targets for intervention, depending on the individual pathways that led to the disorder. For example, for patients with chronic depression and irritable bowel syndrome, it has been demonstrated that those with childhood trauma experiences benefitted from different treatments than those without such experiences.

In conclusion, adopting a developmental neuroscience perspective has significant potential to advance our understanding of CFS. Insights from this line of research may help to overcome the prevailing rejection of the idea that psychological factors may play a role in CFS, at least for a proportion of cases. Perhaps patients and advocacy groups fear to be labeled with the stigma of 'simulating' symptoms, as initially suggested by Freud. However, modern neuroscience clearly demonstrates that experience shapes biology (and *vice versa*) and, in this way, can create 'real' organic symptoms. Freud's legacy is that he was remarkably correct in recognizing that early-life trauma is a major risk factor for a variety of functional disorders. However, it was Hans Selye who realized that successful biological adaptation to stress is critical to maintain health. The key to CFS might lie in the combination of both points of view, based on indisputable advances from modern developmental neuroscience.

CHAPTER 3

Personal Narratives

A Chronic Fatigue Syndrome Sufferer Describes the Problems of Getting Diagnosed

Tamara L. DeGray

Tamara L. DeGray, a college student, wondered for two years why she was so tired and felt so sick, until finally she was diagnosed with chronic fatigue syndrome, a name she hates because it gives people the wrong impression of the characteristics of the illness. She prefers the name chronic fatigue immune dysfunction syndrome (CFIDS) since, in her case, problems with her immune system were found. But prior to that discovery, she saw many doctors and went through a long sequence of medical tests, none of which were positive. For a while it was thought that DeGray had cancer, but her oncologist decided that she did not. At last, her primary care physician told her that since everything else had been ruled out, she must have CFIDS.

This August [2010], after a year of testing and nearly two years of wondering why I was so sick and so tired, I was diagnosed with Chronic Fatigue Immune Dysfunction Syndrome (CFIDS). (Also known by the horrible name of Chronic Fatigue Syndrome (CFS),

SOURCE: Tamara L. DeGray, "CFIDS/CFS/ME: The Illness That's Exhausting Even to Say," tldegray.posterous.com, September 15, 2010. Reproduced by permission.

Photo on facing page. A man with CFS is prepped for an infusion of Ampligen, an experimental drug that stimulates the innate immune system. (Will & Deni McIntyre/Photo Researchers, Inc.)

and as Myalgic Encephalomyelitis or Myalgic Encephalopathy (ME) elsewhere in the world.) I prefer CFIDS because it was the immune dysfunction that was the final clue in my diagnosis, but sometimes I honestly wish we'd call it Myalgic Encephalomyelitis here in the US because at least then disclosure of my illness wouldn't be greeted with skepticism and comments of "yeah, I'm really tired, too."

[According to the Massachusetts CFIDS & ME Association, CFIDS]

> is a complex, debilitating, and often disabling illness which affects multiple systems of the body. Most people with CFIDS experience profound exhaustion, post-exertional malaise, sleep disorder, neurological and flu-like symptoms, and cognitive problems such as difficulty thinking, processing, and remembering. The illness may last many months or years. Symptoms may vary in severity and may wax and wane. There is as yet no known definitive, one cause. It is likely that there are several triggers that set off a cascading panoply of pathological changes in many of the body's systems. While there is no known cure, many of the symptoms can be treated. Some patients show improvement over time, while others may show little improvement or a worsening of symptoms.

Before finding out I had CFIDS I thought I had many different illnesses all at the same time. Because of the huge variety of symptoms it seemed logical that I could have the flu at the same time as I had worsening of my asthma and perimenopause, and that maybe, just maybe, my PHN [post-herpetic neuralgia] was causing my severe exhaustion. But I didn't have the flu, both my primary care doctor and my gynecologist ruled out perimenopause, and, well, nobody really knows what PHN causes, so maybe it does contribute to the fatigue.

I kept getting more and more tired. Now, when I say tired, I don't mean I was yawning and had to get my full eight hours of sleep every night. I mean I sleep over 12 hours each night and still require a 4 hour nap during the day, if not more. Sometimes I sleep for a full day straight. I noticed I was even more tired after doing things. Any things. Going out to dinner, visiting my family, swimming in the pool for 1 hour, sitting in class for three hours, all those things caused me to sleep for 6–8 hours after them and be nearly unable to get out of bed for a day or two after.

Many Tests

We tested for everything. If it in any way could cause these symptoms, we tested for and eliminated it. I don't have Lyme disease, I don't have MS [multiple sclerosis] or Lupus [erythematosus]. My blood sugars are just over the line high but not enough to cause this fatigue and certainly something that could and should have been taken care of with a prescription. We'll be testing for sleep apnea in a few weeks but I'm doubtful that's the issue, and even if it is, [it is] common enough to have that comorbid [simultaneously] with CFIDS.

This past summer was "the summer of infections." First there was the infected cyst which caused me to run a fever from infection. I stayed in bed for nearly a full week after the surgery to clear it, and told myself that even minor outpatient surgery can take it out of you. Then exactly (and I do mean exactly) two weeks later I had strep throat. The doctor who diagnosed it thought the timing was a bit weird, so close to my previous infection, but could see just by looking at how red and raw my throat was that I had an infection. He asked what antibiotics I'd taken the previous week and made sure to prescribe different ones. Then about three and a half weeks after that I was feeling flu-ish again and noticed some swelling in my lymph nodes. Swollen lymph nodes mean infection so I called the doctor and off I went. By the time I got there, one day later, the lymph nodes on the right side of my neck had swelled up into a huge lump running along my jawline, clearly visible just by looking at me. At this point, I wondered if I had some auto-immune disease.

Now, this swollen lymph node thing was scary. The doctor I saw immediately sent me for an ultrasound and they nearly immediately booked me for an MRI [magnetic resonance imaging]. After the MRI, about fifteen minutes before I was supposed to leave the house to take a Spanish final, my doctor called me. She told me to get a pencil and paper. She told me to sit down. Then she told me about cancer. I wrote everything down, I read it all back to her, and I promised to be in touch with her after I saw the Oncologist [cancer specialist] in a week. Then I took my final, numb all the way through.

Later that day I picked up the MRI report and copies of my blood tests to make sure I had them when I saw the Oncologist. (And because my doctor made me promise not to call my family until after I read the reports so I could answer any questions. Being an amazingly wonderful doctor, she also made me promise to tell my Spanish professor what had just happened—I broke down in nervous laughter after she told me the diagnosis and managed to sputter out that I had a final to take—and to have the professor contact her if there was any problem.) I read them, I called my husband and mother, then I rested. A few days later I was ready to read the MRI analysis again and I saw that it said it could indicate cancer (maltoma, scary word) but that it could also indicate long-term infection but that diagnosis was doubtful since "the patient has not been sick."

But I had. I'd been sick all summer long. I sent my doctor a fax reviewing all my infections (they'd been on weekends through the urgent care clinic, not directly through her) and told her that I absolutely wanted to forge ahead and make sure that it wasn't cancer, but I also wanted to make sure we didn't ignore the infection/illness aspect. That was the turning point.

Ruling Out Cancer

The Oncologist was late to my appointment. He apologized, saying he was those few minutes late because he was reading reports from my primary care doctor. She'd told him about all my infections and my concerns. (When I said how wonderful that was that they communicated like that, he told me that was why he moved to my hospital, because it had a reputation for teamwork. An incredible thing for me, that's for sure.) He asked me all sorts of questions about my entire medical history. He told my mother he was thrilled she was there because he needed to know things about my birth, infancy, and childhood health. I told him every symptom I have: the fatigue; the post-exertional malaise; the way I always feel as though I'm coming down with the flu; my chronic sore throat, earache, and cough; my new type of headaches; the way I forget common words; and, yes, my swollen lymph nodes which by the time of this appointment, a week after the MRI and two weeks after the ultrasound, had already shrunk nearly back to normal.

> **FAST FACT**
>
> A study has found that, on average, patients see twelve specialists before being correctly diagnosed with CFS.

He decided to send me to an ENT [ears, nose, and throat specialist] for a laryngoscopy (yes, that is "up your nose with a rubber hose" as the ENT said) and let the ENT decide if we needed a biopsy. He thought they might be able to do one right there, and indeed they were set up for one when I went in a week later. He also took some blood, though he didn't tell me for what and I didn't ask. (I was busy worrying about my sky-high blood pressure and how the Oncologist was calling my primary care physician about it right in front of me. I thought she might come downstairs and make me stay in the hospital until I calmed down! Turns out they just increased my medication and released me to my mother's care, as I was spending the weekend with her anyway.)

A week later, the ENT felt my neck, then looked at my lymph nodes through a tiny little tube. They were swollen but not horribly so, and nowhere near what they had been. He decided a biopsy was not needed and that he'd see me in a month to check. (I've just seen him again and he saw and felt nothing at all unusual about my lymph nodes. I have a follow-up with the Oncologist, an MRI in November [2010], and another follow-up with the ENT to make sure, but it's all looking very good.)

After that initial ENT visit I had occasion to visit my primary care physician yet again. I was getting worse in everything and since it seemed I didn't have cancer, what did I have? We'd already ruled out so many other possibilities. She told me the Oncologist took blood to test for presence of Epstein-Barr Virus and Cytomegalovirus, and that there's evidence that I have been in contact with or had EBV, but that I do not have CMV. Then she told me that based on this and everything else, I have CFIDS.

That made so much sense to me. Every single symptom I have, no matter how weird, can be explained by CFIDS. It is often linked to EBV, and sometimes linked to shingles. Even my weird sore throat and the way the other night I had to pantomime "bag" because I couldn't think of the word can be explained by CFIDS.

I'm not sure yet how I feel about this diagnosis. It's a relief to know, but if you look back up at the [Massachusetts] CFIDS/ME & FM Association definition you'll see that there's no cure. I have a lot of learning to do. It's become important that I treat the symptoms because I cannot treat the disease. It's crucial that I conserve my energy and prioritize every part of my life. I can literally only do so much so I have to make sure I'm doing the important things. I'm not able to work. I'm trying to go to school but it's a tremendous struggle. My life has changed and not for the better.

An Author Adapts to Chronic Fatigue Syndrome by Writing a Best-Selling Book

Michael Shelden

In the following selection, writer Michael Shelden tells the story of Laura Hillenbrand's battle with chronic fatigue syndrome (CFS). For years Hillenbrand did not leave her home and was bedridden for months at a time, yet doctors could find nothing wrong with her. Eventually they diagnosed her CFS, which she believes was triggered by food poisoning when she was nineteen. She was losing hope of ever doing anything with her life until she began researching the life of the famous race-horse Seabiscuit and his jockey, finding information in books and on the Internet and eventually through telephone interviews. She managed to write a book while sitting up in bed or sometimes, for a few hours, at a desk. When she submitted it to a publisher, she did not disclose that she was ill. But the book was a great success and was also made into an Oscar-nominated movie in 2003. Bolstered by her fame and fortune, she has spoken out to raise awareness of CFS. Her illness still keeps her at home, but she has learned to live with it, has married, published another book, and wants to be a mother. Michael Shelden wrote this piece for the *Telegraph*, a British newspaper. He is currently an English professor at Indiana State University.

SOURCE: Laura Hillenbrand, as told to Michael Shelden, "A Dead Horse Rescued Me," *Telegraph* (UK), September 3, 2004. Copyright © Telegraph Media Group Limited 2004. Reproduced by permission of Michael Shelden.

Low on money and suffering from a mysterious, debilitating illness, Laura Hillenbrand thought her life was finished before she was 30.

She hadn't left her house in Washington DC for years and was bedridden for months at a time, her body so emaciated that she couldn't sleep on her side because the bones pressed too hard against her flesh. "I could tell you a lot about the weave of my carpet," she says. "I spent hours staring at it, unable to leave my room."

A series of doctors probed, poked and tested and found nothing, prompting one exasperated female physician to wonder aloud: "When is she going to realise that her problems are all in her head?" Eventually, her disease was diagnosed as chronic fatigue syndrome, triggered, in her case, she believes, by a severe bout of food poisoning when she was 19. But having a name for her illness wasn't much of a consolation—there is no cure and very little understanding of its effects on the body.

"I was losing hope. I had spent so much of my life trapped in bed that I didn't see how I could ever find an escape. I kept asking myself: 'How do I survive?'"

That was seven years ago [1997] and her answer came in the unlikely form of a dead horse. Hillenbrand had always been fascinated by racing and became intrigued by a photograph of the American jockey Red Pollard posing with an arm around his most famous mount, Seabiscuit. She began researching the lives of both horse and rider, using the Internet and borrowed books, and making copious notes as she sat up in bed or worked for a few dizzy hours each day at a nearby desk.

She taught herself to write and earned some freelance assignments by doing interviews over the telephone, then used her extensive research on Seabiscuit to complete her first book. It was a gruelling experience for someone who could barely stand up. The most pernicious of her many symptoms is vertigo, which makes her feel, she says, as though she is riding on the deck of a pitching ship. "It's like everything is moving. The floor gives way, the book-cases ripple, the whole world around me seems to be made of liquid."

But she forced herself to stick to her task, sometimes writing with her eyes closed, propping her feet inside a small refrigerator to moderate her chronic fevers and stacking bowls of cereal near her desk so that she could eat and work without getting up.

"I knew I had to do something to prove to myself that I could have a life apart from my illness. I just had to push myself through the pain. When you have a terrible disease that people don't understand, it defines you and blots out everything else about you. I wanted to create something that would redefine me, that my illness couldn't touch."

Laura Hillenbrand (pictured) coped with her CFS diagnosis by writing a book while confined to her bed. Her book, *Seabiscuit*, became a best-seller. (Bill O'Leary/ **The Washington Post via Getty Images**)

Success as an Author

When the book came out in 2001, it earned immediate praise for its vivid and seemingly authentic portrayal of American horseracing in the 1930s. Most of her bedazzled reviewers had no idea that she was housebound and had never set eyes on any of the places or people featured in her work.

She didn't even tell her editor of her condition, communicating with him by telephone and e-mail and withholding any mention of her disease until after the book was finished.

The trick for her was to pretend that she and her characters inhabited the same world—a sort of parallel reality in which their struggles were hers.

"I was so obsessed and fascinated by my subject that I just left my world behind and entered another one and made it as real as I could. It was the only escape I had available to me. For four or five hours a day, I was lost in that other world and could forget that I was so ill."

She found herself drawn especially to tiny Red Pollard, who was plagued by injuries throughout his riding career—breaking bone after bone in horrific spills and overcoming his injuries by sheer willpower. She wrote her book with his thin, battered face looking down at her from a picture hung above her desk. If he could ignore his pain and ride Seabiscuit to victory, she thought, then there was hope for her. At any rate, she was determined to honour his example by fighting her own literary battle and beating the heavy odds against her.

She had help from her long-time companion, Borden Flanagan, a professor in Washington who has been at her side off and on since her illness began in 1987. He encouraged her ambitions to write and helped support her when money was tight. Her parents—who are divorced—seem to have been less enthusiastic about her obsession with Seabiscuit, and she refers vaguely to "difficulties" between her and her family, which includes three siblings. "I don't like to talk about it," she says, politely.

Now, at 37, fame and fortune have finally found her, bringing considerable royalties from the sales of over seven million copies of *Seabiscuit* worldwide—not to mention a hefty sum from Hollywood's recent film version, starring Jeff Bridges and Tobey Maguire.

Ongoing Illness

But all her success can't break the grip that her illness still exercises over her life. In the immediate aftermath of her book's publication, she suffered a severe relapse and worried that she would never write again.

All the same, there have been some encouraging signs. She has made a few brief efforts to venture beyond her front door, once going on a two-hour car journey for a holiday break to the Maryland shore. But it was a major undertaking and left her so exhausted that she needed days to recover.

A more promising—but rather odd—episode concerns her recent appearance in a magazine ad, extolling the virtues of Pond's facial cream. Despite her long history of poor health, the marketing people at Pond's saw her face in publicity photos and liked her delicate features. They asked her to pose for their cameras, she agreed and a make-up artist was dispatched to her house. "I enjoyed it," she says, adding in a modest tone, "they made me feel so pretty."

There aren't many debilitating illnesses that allow you to write long books of history and appear in ads for beauty creams, but Hillenbrand insists that her problems are real and have plagued her for almost half her life because something in her body—not her mind—has turned against her.

"The disease is relentless. You don't get better. But you can learn to live with it. I have become more at peace with myself as a sick person. I used to hate myself for causing everyone so much trouble, but I'm learning to forgive myself. It's not my fault. It's something that has taken over my body."

Hoping for a Family

Far from surrendering to her malady, she has now declared her intention not only to proceed with another book—an epic story of Louis Zamperini, the war hero and Olympic runner of the Thirties—but also to marry her companion and start a family.

For years, her illness made her rule out any chance of having a child. What changed her mind was her success. She is more confident of herself and now has the money to hire a nanny, an unimaginable luxury before her book came out.

FAST FACT

Among the well-known people besides Laura Hillenbrand who have chronic fatigue syndrome are speed skater Amy Peterson, US women's soccer star Michelle Akers, former Styx member Dennis DeYoung, jazz pianist Keith Jarrett, and British composer/conductor John Rutter.

But she also is holding out a strong hope that pregnancy itself might be just the bodily change needed to counteract whatever triggered her illness in the first place. It's a risky thought. She knows it, yet sees so much hope in it and doesn't want to lose another chance to make the most of her restricted existence.

"I want children. Many people with this illness get a lot better when they're pregnant. For one thing, it increases blood volume. As for bringing up children, we can manage. There are ways to make these things work."

Perhaps she is right. But first, she needs to escape long enough from the house to get married. She is hoping to have a simple ceremony at a quiet little church in the neighbourhood and is cautiously making plans.

In the meantime, she is sticking as close to her front door as ever and is stacking up the cereal boxes on her desk for another rigorous attempt to steady the pitching ship of her life.

She sounds remarkably cheery about the difficulties facing her. "It's not as bad as it could be, staying home and doing my kind of work. If I were an archaeologist, I'd really be in trouble."

[*Editor's note:* Laura Hillenbrand married Borden Flanagan in 2008. Her new book was published in 2010.]

An Astrophysicist Explains What It Is Like to Have Myalgic Encephalomyelitis

P.S.B.

The author of this narrative was a member of the committee that in 2008 made recommendations for US government policy toward chronic fatigue syndrome. Her story was included in the committee's official report, along with those of the other members, to make clear how debilitating myalgic encephalomyelitis/chronic fatigue syndrome (ME/CFS) is and how seriously it disrupts people's lives. P.S.B. was an astrophysicist whose career ended, she says, when she was disabled by illness and became unable to work. For a while she could barely walk, using canes, and she still cannot stand up for long without fainting. She was unable to speak more than a few words at first and can read very little. She also has great difficulty remembering events. She has lost her friends, except for those she meets through support groups, and she finds the social isolation frightening. The lack of support for ME/CFS from the government, she says, makes her depressed and angry.

SOURCE: P.S.B., "Personal Stories," *Obama-Biden Transition Project Health Care Community Discussion Report*, December 30, 2008. Reproduced by permission of the author.

I have been disabled by M.E. [myalgic encephalomyelitis] longer than I worked as a productive member of society. I am an astrophysicist, but spent the bulk of my short career working in computer telecommunications. Before moving back to my family home in Alabama, I lived in the Northeastern US, primarily the Washington area. That is where I sought treatment for this new disease when I became ill, and found that there was no treatment that worked. During the years I lingered there trying to find medical help, I became involved with the CFS [chronic fatigue syndrome] Coordinating Committee, now called the CFSAC [Chronic Fatigue Syndrome Advisory Committee]. . . .

I was struck down at the age of 40, while working as a consultant for the federal government on communication interoperability issues, in November, 1989. In my case, I had an extreme viral onset that was like a severe case of influenza; it was like Texas flu or Swine flu, both of which I had during the years in which they were pandemic. As usual, there was supreme difficulty in obtaining a diagnosis. My knowledge of this disease was nil at that time. For all I knew, I had Lyme disease, or hepatitis, or any of a very large number of viruses I was tested for. I was finally diagnosed by an infectious diseases specialist who used the CDC [Centers for Disease Control and Prevention] 1988 definition of CFS, through a process of elimination. I've come to know a lot about what I now know is Myalgic Encephalomyelitis due to brute force exposure to it.

A Disabling Illness

What is it like to have Myalgic Encephalomyelitis? There are physical, cognitive, and social as well as emotional aspects that have happened in my case; we are all different, for this disease has "different results after inflicting the same insult" upon us. That is a phrase I learned probably 15 years ago from a fellow activist in the Washington, D.C. area. Here is a little glimpse of how my life crumbled from what was once a promising career at the top of a group of enterprising people who were planning for "Battlefield 2005 telecommunications," to what I am now, a broken woman who can barely string sentences together.

I have been totally unable to work since 1991, and have been disabled since that time. I lost my job. My legs literally went out from under me and I had to undergo lengthy physical therapy while using 2 canes to walk, haltingly and for only short distances. I walk much better now, after several courses of therapy, including two at facilities of the Warm Springs Institute in Georgia. There are times when I stand too long, and I begin to black out. I can avoid fainting if I sit down, and I will sometimes sit down in a public place on the floor rather than risk fainting. Other physical problems include the onset of fibromyalgia, and several organ system diseases which may be related to the autonomic nervous system aspect of M.E. Since I don't know if they are cause-and-effect, I don't relate them here, but I have become more-or-less bed bound, with only two to four hours of activity per day.

Early in the disease, for some months, I was unable to speak more than a few words. I can usually carry on a conversation now; my self-retraining in what I call word retrieval has been compared to what a stroke victim goes through. Still, I frequently have to close my eyes to remember words though. Reading the printed word became a thing of the past. I can now read a few sentences at a time, but my retention is very poor. I listen to audio books now, and I like to joke that I can listen to the same mystery novel over and over because I don't remember the end. In the past 6 years, I've also developed permanent visual dysfunction too, called palinopsia, which makes it nearly

> **FAST FACT**
>
> On December 6, 2010, the ME/CFS Worldwide Patient Alliance, a grassroots organization, placed a half-page ad in the *Washington Post* emphasizing the potential danger posed by the XMRV virus and appealing for more research funding.

impossible to drive at night, and makes reading from a computer screen much more difficult.

Memory is a very tricky problem now. I have a sort of sliding window of time in the recent past during which I can remember events. It may be 3 days ago up to 6 months ago, or the window may shut down at 3 weeks. I never know if I am going to remember an event, an appointment, or a person. In fact, I have more or less given up on people recognition; unless I see someone daily or maybe weekly, I do not recognize the face. The only reason I know about this sliding memory window is that I have lived with my sister for several years, and she has described it to me. I keep track of appointments and such on my cell phone calendar, without which I would never be able to meet any of my obligations. This technology has helped me tremendously in the last few years.

I've written this memory description down and keep it for whenever I need to explain it to people, like doctors. Or, as in for this description of my condition for our input to the policy makers for President-elect [Barack] Obama.

Social Isolation

Maybe it is not obvious, but in becoming this ill and unable to function at any sort of professional level, I lost the friends that I had made throughout the years in my field. I lost track of my friends that I had still kept up with in academia, because I was still living in the same northeastern megalopolis where we had been friends. My extreme inability to travel—energy deficits, the need for frequent stops to sit or lie down, and other problems that are poorly understood by healthy people—also cut me off from many of my dearest friends, including my most 'significant other.' I stopped making new friends, unless they were sick like me and I got to know them through support group meetings, or in attending government committee meetings. Even then, I usually lost track of them (unless I made a photograph—I learned that was an important tool) due to memory problems and lack of functional time during each day.

Social isolation has become probably the most frightening aspect of living with M.E. The physical symptoms can only make you sick or dead. But isolation makes you miserable every hour of your day. It never ends. Of course this is true for all chronic illnesses, but M.E. is so poorly understood by everyone who does not have it, it's not even possible to get a fair hearing from one's pastor or an organization that is intended to insure against isolation. Socially speaking, I am living in a dead zone.

My own family cannot find their way to an understanding of what has happened to me. I live in my own home, a huge house that I cannot clean, and cannot afford to hire people to clean or to take care of the lawn. So I am always attempting—and always unsuccessfully—to do those chores myself. The result—a feeling of self loathing because I can't do what I should be able to do. After being sick for almost 20 years, I still try to do what is of course impossible and act like I'm not sick.

That's irrational. So finally, there is the emotional part of this disease. I don't say that I never feel depressed, but I'm not clinically depressed. What I am is just what the book title said: *Sick and Tired of Being Sick and Tired.* Angry that the people I have trusted to find out what is wrong with me and to find out how to treat it, took the money and misused it; they stole my trust. They might as well have stolen my life. Afraid that I will never feel well enough to accomplish any of the things I had set aside in my younger years to do after I climbed my big career mountain. Afraid I will never again enjoy life like I did 21 years ago.

It took me several days to pull these few pages together, from material that I mostly already had written. . . . I hope it will give some insight into what living with M.E. is like, and why we who have the disease cannot rest until our few short pleas are met by our elected officials.

GLOSSARY

CDC   The Centers for Disease Control and Prevention, the US government agency in the Department of Health and Human Services responsible for the investigation, control, and prevention of disease.

central nervous system   The brain and spinal cord.

CFIDS   Chronic fatigue and immune dysfunction syndrome; another name for chronic fatigue syndrome (CFS) preferred by some patients and organizations. Whether CFS is an immune disorder is controversial.

comorbid conditions   Medical conditions that exist simultaneously in a person but are usually independent of each other.

cytokines   Proteins produced by certain types of lymphocytes that are important controllers of immune functions.

Epstein-Barr virus (EBV)   A virus in the herpes family that causes mononucleosis. CFS was at one time thought to be a chronic infection with EBV.

fibromyalgia   A disorder closely related to CFS whose major symptoms include pain, tenderness, and muscle stiffness, in addition to some of the symptoms common in CFS; many patients have both CFS and fibromyalgia.

hypochondriac   A person who is abnormally concerned about his or her health and frequently experiences imaginary illnesses; people with CFS are often suspected of being hypochondriacs before finding a doctor who correctly diagnoses their condition.

ICD   *The International Classification of Diseases*, an official document issued by the World Health Organization in which ME/CFS is classified as a neurological disease. *See* myalgic encephalomyelitis (ME).

lymph nodes	Small immune system organs containing lymphocytes that are found in the neck, armpits, groin, and other locations in the body.
lymphocytes	White blood cells that are responsible for the actions of the immune system.
mononucleosis	A flu-like illness caused by the Epstein-Barr virus, often called simply *mono.*
myalgia	Muscle pain.
myalgic encephalomyelitis (ME)	A disease characterized, as its name denotes, by muscle pain and inflammation of the brain and spinal cord; often used interchangeably with CFS, especially in the United Kingdom and Europe. Its use in the United States is increasing, apparent in the growing use of the abbreviation *ME/CFS.* Many, though, believe the two to be separate diseases because CFS sufferers do not usually have the inflammation of the brain and spinal cord.
natural killer cell	A lymphocyte that acts as a primary immune defense against infection; sometimes, mainly in Japan, CFS is known as low natural killer cell syndrome.
neurally mediated hypotension	A rapid fall in blood pressure that causes dizziness, blurred vision, and fainting, and is often followed by prolonged fatigue.
neurasthenia	Nervous exhaustion; a disorder commonly diagnosed in the late 1800s, presenting symptoms of irritability and weakness and now thought to have been CFS.
neurology	The scientific study of the nervous system, which consists of the brain, spinal cord, nerves, and receptor organs.
postexertional malaise	Extreme exhaustion and a general feeling of being unwell that lasts for more than a day following physical exertion.
post-viral fatigue syndrome	Another name for CFS used by the World Health Organization.
psychosomatic	Actual physical effects on the body caused by psychological or emotional factors but often used erroneously to refer to imagined symptoms.

retrovirus A special kind of virus with genetic material consisting of RNA that reproduces by transcribing itself into DNA that then inserts itself into a host's cells.

somatization Unconscious conversion of a psychological state such as anxiety or depression into physical symptoms for which there is no biological cause.

syndrome A collection of signs, symptoms, and medical problems that tend to occur together but are not related to a specific, identifiable cause.

WHO World Health Organization, the directing and coordinating authority for health within the United Nations system.

XAND X-associated neuroimmune disease: A name for CFS proposed by researchers who believe that it is caused by the XMRV virus.

XMRV virus Xenotropic murine leukemia virus–related virus, a retrovirus recently found to be present in the blood of some CFS patients and suspected as a cause of CFS.

Yuppie flu A name formerly applied by the media to CFS, reflecting the mistaken idea that it affects mainly young, affluent people; the term is considered offensive by patients and doctors.

CHRONOLOGY

1869   An illness with symptoms similar to chronic fatigue syndrome is named *neurasthenia*, from the Greek meaning "nerve weakness," which becomes a common diagnosis in the late nineteenth century. In the twentieth century neurasthenia is increasingly thought to be a behavioral rather than a physical disorder.

1938   The term *myalgic encephalomyelitis* (ME) first appears in medical literature.

1956   ME is first defined in an editorial by A. Melvin Ramsay published in the British medical journal the *Lancet*.

1969   Myalgic encephalomyelitis is first recognized by the World Health Organization (WHO), which classifies it as a neurological disorder.

1984   The first documented clusters of CFS-like cases in the United States occur near Lake Tahoe, Nevada, and in Lyndonville, New York.

1985   The National Institute of Allergy and Infectious Diseases holds a conference at which the name *chronic Epstein-Barr virus* (CEBV) is used, and medical journals begin referring to CEBV as a legitimate illness.

1987   The term *chronic fatigue syndrome* (CFS) first appears in medical literature in reference to an illness resembling CEBV but with no evidence of being caused by the Epstein-Barr virus; the CEBV Association, which later changes its name to The CFIDS Association of America (TCAA), is founded. It prefers the name CFIDS (chronic fatigue and immune dysfunction syndrome) to CFS because it more accurately indicates the seriousness of the illness.

1988   The first case definition of the illness is issued by the federal Centers for Disease Control (CDC), which decides on *chronic fatigue syndrome* as its official name.

1990   The term *Yuppie flu* is popularized in a *Newsweek* cover story, which promotes a false stereotype about CFS patients and leads to a public perception that the illness is merely psychological.

1993   A panel of scientists formed by the CDC considers arguments for changing the name of the illness but decides that since its cause is unknown a name change would be premature. Patients, angry over the use of a name that suggests the disease is insignificant, continue to seek the change during subsequent years.

1994   New diagnostic criteria for CFS are proposed by the CDC. They are sometimes called the "Fukuda definition" after the first author of the publication in which they are proposed. Although developed for research purposes, they are nonetheless officially used for diagnosis.

1995   The first congressional briefings about CFS are held, and the US Department of Health and Human Services adds patient advocates to its CFS Coordinating Committee.

1998   A code for CFS is included in the WHO's International Classification of Diseases (ICD) under the category "Signs, Symptoms and Ill-Defined Conditions."

1999   The Social Security Administration recognizes CFS as a potentially disabling condition.

1999   The CDC's misuse of $12.9 million in funds intended by Congress for CFS research is confirmed after an investigation by the US inspector general; the agency issues a public apology, and Congress agrees to restore the funds.

2001   Laura Hillenbrand achieves fame as the author of the best-selling book *Seabiscuit* and begins to talk publicly about her living with CFS, thereby increasing awareness of the illness.

2003   A case definition for CFS developed for clinical, rather than research purposes, is adopted in Canada; it is known as the Canadian Consensus Criteria and is preferred by some doctors and patients in the United States as well.

2006   The CDC acknowledges that CFS is a serious illness and launches a public awareness campaign.

2009   Genetic changes affecting response to exercise are found in people with CFS as compared with healthy people, indicating that the illness has a biological basis.

     News reports of a study that found the XMRV virus in the blood of CFS patients result in a heated controversy when other studies fail to show the same result.

2010   A new study confirms the association between the XMRV virus and CFS, although the issue remains controversial. The American Red Cross bars CFS patients from donating blood; the Chronic Fatigue Syndrome Advisory Committee of the US Department of Health and Human Services unanimously endorses a recommendation that the government change the name *CFS* to *ME/CFS*.

ORGANIZATIONS TO CONTACT

The editors have compiled the following list of organizations concerned with the issues debated in this book. The descriptions are derived from materials provided by the organizations. All have publications or information available for interested readers. The list was compiled on the date of publication of the present volume; the information provided here may change. Be aware that many organizations take several weeks or longer to respond to inquiries, so allow as much time as possible.

Association of Young People with ME (AYME)
10 Vermont Pl.
Tongwell, Milton
Keynes, MK15 8JA, UK
e-mail: info@ayme.org
.uk
website: www.ayme.org
.uk

AYME is a British organization for children and young adults with myalgic encephalomyelitis/chronic fatigue syndrome (ME/CFS). Although focused on members in the UK, its website includes information and advice appropriate for interested teens anywhere.

Centers for Disease Control and Prevention (CDC)
1600 Clifton Rd.
Atlanta, GA 30333
(800) 232-4636
e-mail: cdcinfo@cdc
.gov
website: www.cdc.gov/
cfs

The CDC is a US government agency in the Department of Health and Human Services. The "Chronic Fatigue Syndrome"(CFS) section of its website contains extensive information about CFS, its possible causes, treatment options, and research conducted by the agency.

Chronic Fatigue and Immune Dysfunction Syndrome Association of America (CFIDS)
PO Box 220398,
Charlotte, NC 28222
(704) 365-2343
e-mail: cfids@cfids.org
website: www.cfids.org

The CFIDS is the largest and most active nonprofit organization dedicated to CFS. It works to stimulate research aimed at the early detection, objective diagnosis, and effective treatment of CFS through expanded public, private, and commercial investment. Its website offers extensive information on medical and political issues related to CFS, including a page for young people, plus many personal stories of patients. It also contains archives of its four publications: *SolveCFS, CFIDSLink*, the *CFIDS Chronicle*, and the *Research Review*.

National CFIDS Foundation (NCF)
103 Aletha Rd.
Needham, MA 02492
(781) 449-3535
fax: (781) 449-8606
e-mail: info@ncf-net
.org
website: www.ncf-net
.org

The NCF is a nonprofit organization whose objective is to fund research to find a cause, expedite treatments, and eventually find a cure for CFIDS, as well as providing information, education, and support to people who have CFIDS. Its website contains news and information about research it has funded, plus many technical articles about related medical issues. Its newsletter, except for a few online articles, is available only to subscribers.

National Chronic Fatigue Syndrome and Fibromyalgia Association (NCFSFA)
PO Box 18426, Kansas City, MO 64133
(816) 737-1343
website: www.ncfsfa
.org

The NCFSFA is a nonprofit organization whose mission is to educate and inform the public about the nature and impact of chronic fatigue syndrome and fibromyalgia and related disorders. Its website contains news and informational articles for both patients and physicians about these illnesses and their management.

Nightingale Research Foundation
121 Iona St., Ottawa
ON K1Y 3M1 Canada
e-mail: info@nightin
gale.ca
website: www.nightin
gale.ca

The Nightingale Research Foundation is a nonprofit Canadian organization dedicated to the study and treatment of myalgic encephalomyelitis and chronic fatigue syndrome and related illnesses. It collaborates with other medical organizations worldwide and disseminates information to researchers, to the legal and advocate community, to health-care professionals, and to patients and their caregivers. Its website focuses on material written by its founder, Dr. Byron Hyde, who believes that the official definitions of ME and CFS are seriously flawed.

FOR FURTHER READING

Books

Alex Barton, *Recovery from CFS: 50 Personal Stories.* Bloomington, IN: AuthorHouse, 2008.

Tami Brady, *Strategies: A Chronic Fatigue Syndrome and Fibromyalgia Journey.* Ann Arbor, MI: Loving Healing Press, 2008.

Frankie Campling and Michael Sharpe, *Chronic Fatigue Syndrome (CFS/ME).* New York: Oxford University Press, 2008.

Rik Carlson, *We're Not in Kansas Anymore: Chronic Fatigue Syndrome and the Politics of Disease.* Burlington, VT: Monkeys with Wings, 2004.

Celeste Cooper and Jeffrey Miller, *Integrative Therapies for Fibromyalgia, Chronic Fatigue Syndrome, and Myofascial Pain: The Mind-Body Connection.* Rochester, VT: Healing Arts Press, 2010.

Hillary Johnson, *Osler's Web: Inside the Labyrinth of the Chronic Fatigue Syndrome Epidemic.* New York: Backinprint.com, 2006.

Susan R. Lisman and Karla Dougherty, *Chronic Fatigue Syndrome for Dummies.* Hoboken, NJ: Wiley, 2007.

Anne MacIntyre and Clare Francis, *M.E.: Chronic Fatigue Syndrome: A Practical Guide.* London: Thorson's, 2009.

Lorraine Steefel, *What Nurses Know: Chronic Fatigue Syndrome.* New York: Demos Medical, 2010.

Edita Svoboda and Kristof Zelenjcik, *Chronic Fatigue Syndrome: Symptoms, Causes and Prevention.* New York: Nova Biomedical, 2010.

Dorothy Wall, *Encounters with the Invisible: Unseen Illness, Controversy, and Chronic Fatigue Syndrome.* Dallas: Southern Methodist University Press, 2005.

Periodicals

Nicholas Bakalar, "For Chronic Fatigue, Placebos Fail the Test," *New York Times*, March 29, 2005.

B. Bower, "Sick and Tired: Tracking Paths to Chronic Fatigue," *Science News*, November 11, 2006.

Mary A. Fischer, "You Think You're Tired? There's Ordinary, Everyday Tired. And Then There's Dizzy, Feverish, Might-as-Well-Be-Dead Tired," *O, The Oprah Magazine*, September 2006.

Denise Grady, "Virus Is Found in Many with Chronic Fatigue Syndrome," *New York Times*, October 8, 2009.

Denise Grady, "Is a Virus the Cause of Chronic Fatigue Syndrome?," *New York Times*, October 12, 2009.

Healthcare Traveler, "Psychologists: Child Abuse Can Lead to Chronic Pain Later," February 2010.

Laura Hillenbrand, "A Sudden Illness," *New Yorker*, July 7, 2003.

Hillary Johnson, "A Case of Chronic Denial," *New York Times*, October 21, 2009.

Claudia Kalb, "Validation in a Virus?," *Newsweek*, December 6, 2010.

Nancy G. Klimas, "It's Not in Your Head," *Ms.*, Winter 2010.

Amanda MacMillan, "Fatigue Findings," *Prevention*, April 2007.

Eric Nagourney, "Vital Signs: Hormone Levels and Chronic Fatigue," *New York Times*, January 29, 2008.

Nathan Seppa, "Pathogen Fingered as a Potential Culprit in Chronic Fatigue Syndrome," *Science News*, November 7, 2009.

David Tuller, "Chronic Fatigue No Longer Seen as 'Yuppie Flu,'" *New York Times*, July 17, 2007.

David Tuller, "Study Links Chronic Fatigue to Virus Class," *New York Times*, August 24, 2010.

David Tuller, "Exhausted by Illness and Doubts," *New York Times*, January 3, 2011.

Women's Health Weekly, "Scientists at University of Miami Release New Data on Chronic Fatigue Syndrome," March 11, 2010.

INDEX